LOVE AT FIRST FLIGHT

... A Plane Fairytale

David Z. and Tierney Foster-Abel

Gabriel Press USA

Copyright © 2016 by David Z. and Tierney Foster-Abel

Library of Congress Cataloging-in-Publication Data

Abel, David Z. and Tierney Foster-
     Love at first flight . . . . .
     ISBN 978-1-941296-10-3

Scripture texts used in this work are taken from the Holy Bible:

Scripture quotations marked, "AMP," are taken from the Amplified® Bible, Copyright © 2016 by The Lockman Foundation (www.Lockman.org).

Scriptures quotations marked, "NABRE," are taken from the New American Bible (Revised Edition), Copyright © 2010, 1991, 1986, 1970 Confraternity of Christian Doctrine, Inc., Washington, D.C. All rights reserved.

Scripture quotations marked, "NIV," are taken from the Holy Bible, New International Version®, NIV®, Copyright © 1973, 1978, 1984, 2011 by Biblica, Inc.® All rights reserved worldwide (www.zondervan.com). The "NIV" and "New International Version" are trademarks registered in the United States Patent and Trademark Office by Biblica, Inc.®

Scripture quotations marked, "NKJV," are taken from the New King James Version,® Copyright © 1982 by Thomas Nelson. All rights reserved.

Scripture quotations marked, "KJV," are taken from the King James Version.

Scripture quotations marked, "TLB," are taken from The Living Bible, Copyright © 1971. Tyndale House Publishers, Inc., Carol Stream, Illinois 60188. All rights reserved.

Scripture quotations marked, "NLV," are taken from the New Life Version, © Christian Literature International.

Cover design by 68 Creative Group.

Printed in the United States of America

Gabriel Press USA
111 Peyton Avenue
Chicago Heights, IL 60411
www.gabrielpressusa.com

Once in awhile,
right in the middle
of ordinary life,
love gives us
a
Fairy Tale

As I (Tierney) considered writing a book about what lavish love the Father was pouring out, the following text message from David sealed the deal! The book must be written.

> "*Treasured, cherished, and precious are the memories I have stored in the vault of my heart of us. Their value is priceless because money can neither buy nor replace them. Their significance has no earthly measure but rather, a heavenly origin. Books will be written to tell our story, my love. They will impact countless numbers as their message of hope, healing, redemption, and true love, as it was meant to be, pierces the heart of the reader. I love you, my beloved. Thank you, Father, for entrusting to me the heart of Your most precious daughter.*"

> *June 6, 2011*

Table of Contents

ACKNOWLEDGEMENT

[5]Beauty Will Rise
Words and Music by Steven Curtis Chapman
Copyright (c) 2009 One Blue Petal Music
All Rights Administered by BMG Rights Management (US) LLC
All Rights Reserved. Used by Permission.
Reprinted by Permission of Hal Leonard Corporation

PART I

Her Story—Her Capsules and Nuggets Along the Journey

Fear not, nor be afraid [in the coming violent upheavals]; have I not told it to you from of old and declared it? And you are my witnesses! Is there a God besides Me? There is no [other] Rock; I know not any. Isaiah 44:8 AMP

GOD LAID OUT this verse to me and I said, "No! Don't say it!" I shut my Bible quickly and said, "If this is Your Word to me, You can repeat it." Within a week, the verse hit me in the face! What was looming in my future?

I endured almost two years of violent upheavals, starting with a smear and slander campaign from a former associate on our real estate team: A ruthless, relentless, and poisonous verbal attack against my core character and privacy. I stayed, more or less, in a foxhole—lying low until the destruction passed.

The losses I experienced included two short sales on my properties (including my beloved Palm Island property), a marital separation (on Easter Sunday) after 35 years of togetherness, leaving the church I had attended for over 26 years, the alienation of my tender-hearted boys as they grieved and protected themselves, saying goodbye to my son who left to tour with Youth With A Mission, and then returning only to move to Los Angeles. I experienced the loss of revenue and income that came as a result of the market crash and marital separation. As if the market hadn't been enough drain, change, and drama for me, I changed companies after being the top real estate agent for nine years. I transferred to a company in need of systems and leadership. After about a year as the top agent, I experienced loss of significance, placement, and unfounded gossip, slander, accusations, and presumptions. Even after my sacrificial investments, there was a rebel-rousing nucleus of existing staff with a vehement desire to destroy me with their tongues. Not only that, but once-trusted friends maligned me publicly. My tottering foundation attempted to find resolve and reason. An aged "best friend" who was failing after 14 years as my companion dog brought waves of grief in the wings. And believe it or not, there was more! In summary, *I have a heart that is rendered broken, neglected, and refused. Hope deferred makes the heart sick, but a longing fulfilled is a tree of life* (Proverbs 13:12 NIV).

If I could have uttered Jesus's words at the time, I would have said, "Father . . . take this cup from me; yet not my will, but yours be done" (Luke 22:42 NIV).

I must dream, hope, and continue to care. I must find a way through and out of the maze with my Father's protection, and trust His mysterious ways.

Violent Upheaval Update—One Year Later

A<small>FTER THREE-AND-A-HALF YEARS</small> of an agonizing process, my cottage in North Carolina sold in a short sale, miraculously closing within two weeks from approval. This constituted both the quickest and the longest short sale in history! After foreclosure dates, a rejected contract, and finding myself out of agreeable time frames for a *Deed in Lieu* (with two-and-a-half years of marketing within every possible avenue), it was *solely* God's favor that secured a *Deed in Lieu* with my Palm Island property. This was truly a gift out of nowhere!

Together, I received two 1099's from my bank, equaling almost $200,000. I was then notified that there were enough write-offs to nullify any IRS ramifications! This was a miracle.

K.C., my beautiful Siberian husky was painfully "put down." The loss was acute. The boys reached back and embraced me, although one son moved to L.A. and the other moved to the mission field.

My previous husband continued to be "invisible," except when he was invited back for the holidays or for *bon voyage* send-offs, with me initiating the opportunities. His commitment to file for divorce eight months earlier was finally being realized over the three-year process of separation. I patiently waited and prayed. The yokes of devastation were being lifted piece by piece. It appeared that there was no trace of God's deliverance; it was relegated as "nonexistent." However, through it all, the quiet voice of God seemed silent, but His scourging said to me, "Stand and invoke the Word of God to be your comfort and your hope." Those words, in time, were deeply rooted in me. The warfare continued in the area of finances and fears for the future. My empty, agonizing cries from deep within felt hollow and without promise. The prospect of working as hard as ever to rebuild my wealth and security seemed ominous. I faced the realization of the possibility that I could lose my house *and* live alone the rest of my life. The alienation and loss of significance in the office was a daily experience and struggle. Purpose was blighted with hopelessness and a sense of indifference to the query of whether or not I cared to live. Two years felt like a lifetime of "rape" in the market center. Disposed of all hopes for potential positive outcomes, I began believing that the enemy of God's calling on my life had snatched it away. God spoke to my heart, telling me to push past hope and dream. The Holy Spirit said that if I was going to survive, I must worship with as much intensity as I needed to breathe. Rather laboriously, I would try to rise from the deep water, but the surf would overwhelm me and knock me down.

About this time, my aging mother had a stroke. I made daily trips to the rehabilitation center for one month. She was going to require 24/7 care. I was her power of attorney and decision maker. At my lowest ebb, my siblings dropped innuendoes that mom rework her will and have their attorney rescript what she had prescribed several years before.

The changes in her ability to manage her future, and the fact that it was now in my hands, unearthed them and undermined me. During this time, challenges in the office and my business partnership created such insecurity and uncertainty in me that I often plotted to leave both. Mom chose to retain her previous will and elected to move into my home. Over a year passed, and God's kind provision allowed my brother-in-law to care for her by day. My caretaking tasks occurred on evenings and weekends. The reflective feeling of having waited my entire adult life and marriage for someone to lead me, for real life and passion to begin, was fleeting. This new "mom" task brought another degree of responsibility. I "inherited" mom's dog and the care of her two homes. I verbalized, "Lord, just 'load' me up!"

Except for my business partner, I felt so alone and inconspicuously hiding in the foxholes, awaiting "the rescue." The rescue did not surface. Friends seemed to circle, but no one could save me. "How long, oh Lord, will you allow me to be battered from within and from without? How long until you bring deliverance?" He was quiet. I was obedient. *Be still and know that I am God* (Psalm 46:10 NIV). *Sit still, my daughter, until you learn how the matter turns out* (Ruth 3:18 AMP). These are some of the scriptures the Holy Spirit whispered to me. At the beginning of the year, with fasting and groaning, the "curse" at work was lifted. The opposition and enemies were scattered so that peace and order could resume. Things quieted with my siblings, but continued to be disengaging. The load rested on my shoulders, but with the grace of God and at my darkest times and hours, God orchestrated some prophetic words for me that alluded that a new springtime was coming. I had been in winter. (I actually thought it was my task to personally rewrite the Book of Job!) A blossom of hope began to sprout. Anticipation in my spirit started its rebirth, and God used songs of worship to allow me to "pour out" as their power began to resonate from deep within. I identified with the eagle that always flew above the rest—the aging eagle chose to live, and therefore set itself apart in isolation for a lengthy time in order to break its ingrown beak which quelled its ability to hunt. Thus, this desolate time allowed the new beak to grow back ever so slowly. Following the painful process, the once championed eagle plucks out its tattered, oily, and heavy feathers in order for new growth to occur which allows it to fly and hunt again. This seemingly endless process has its purpose in the period of isolation. My beak is back, my talons are apparent, and once again, my wings are stretched for flight.

Love at First Flight—A Plane Fairytale

Okay, okay, I'll go to the Keller Williams' convention in February in Anaheim, California! Yes, I would be honored to be on the Luxury panel of three with Laurie Moore-Moore, renowned Luxury Home Marketing instructor. What an honor! But fly alone? Stay alone? Find my way? Gulp! Cover all bases at work and at home so my clients and mom are taken care of? Whew! That was almost too much work. Maybe I would not go after all—it's easier to stay home. However, it is unbelievable to be asked to share the microphone with the likes of Laurie Moore-Moore. My massage therapist was giving me a massage and intuitively said, "You need to go! Something's going to happen, and you must go!" Hmmm! What does he perceive that I do not? "Okay!" Thinking out loud, I said, "I do get to go and see my son in L.A. for a few days and that will be worthwhile to see his world, encourage him to stay the course, and also meet the people he stays with." I'm settled in now! I'm going!

My business partner orchestrated my tickets, seats, and hotels in and out of Anaheim, California. Realizing later that it would be best to fly out of Los Angeles International Airport after visiting my son, we attempted to change flight locations; however, it would cost too much and be difficult to re-construct. Thus, the show goes on as originally planned.

Following a lonely, but effective speaking experience, I spent precious little time with my son. At 5:00 a.m., on February 26, we left my son's house. I arrived at the John Wayne International Airport (an hour away), in time to fly out around 7:00 a.m. I felt weary, a bit empty, and disheveled. I was heading home to Florida to take care of business, both in my personal life and in my career. I was situated with a favored window seat. I plopped my gear down on the middle seat next to me, hoping that no one was assigned to it so that I could remain isolated, cocooning while reviewing my notes from the seminars and mentally preparing for the challenges ahead. As the plane filled, a gentleman stood in the aisle and said, "Young lady, may I take that seat?" Much to my chagrin, he was assigned to sit next to me. Much to his chagrin, he was assigned to an unusual middle seat, when his preference was always, I would later learn, the less confining aisle seat. Alas, not this time! Destiny wrote a different story. God's fingerprint later showed itself "planely."

Noting that my neighboring seat companion, "David," wore no wedding ring, and was carrying a Catholic-titled book, I thought to myself, 'This will be interesting. Maybe he's a priest! Poor guy! He's probably not going to get to read that book if he's sitting next to me!' Sad, but true. It's not that I like chatting with my neighbor on a plane. It's just what I do. So we exchanged greetings, a few introductory questions, passed business cards, etc. I was surprised to receive two business cards—both ministry cards. One was related to an Ethiopian mission foundation, and the other was related to a "Stewardship" ministry. Hmmmm! Ambitious soul—like me! His name was David Z. Abel. David asked a few questions about my trip and I explained the hows and whys. He explained that he was attending a CEO conference of 1,000 Christian business owners in San Diego. I later learned that he was the recipient of an award they were giving, and he felt obligated to go so he would not disappoint anyone. He flew out one day and returned the next. Neither one of us wanted to be on that plane! I figured out then that he did something else for his livelihood. My sensitive, yet inquisitive nature kicked in. Respectfully, I asked questions—apparently more questions than I realized. David told me about his daughter, Brittany, who was killed in a car accident, for whom the foundation, "Brittany's Hope," was named. I discovered that Brittany's Hope Foundation supports orphanages in Vietnam, Africa, and other countries. As we talked, I learned that this man had 15 children! Twelve were adopted from around the world, and three were "birth" children. Okay, so now I knew that he wasn't a priest, he owned a business, and he was married without a wedding ring! So I said, "Your wife must be a saint!" He candidly explained that he had been separated for over two years. David's "Damascus Road Experience" was vulnerably explained to me as he unlocked his past, exposing his "BC" (Before Christ) sins, failures, abuses, and addictions. He was so articulate that I was a bit embarrassed and certainly thought he should be! With boldness, he shared his last six-plus years: his conversion, his rejections, pains, and devastations. I was amazed that this was our *first* conversation! I learned about his experience and his walk with God, not about his successes or even his notoriety. At one point, he referenced his property. I mentioned that it sounded like he had acreage. Indeed! He owned 275 acres. The rest of the details would unfold in the next few weeks and months. I told him to send me some pictures of his property. I learned that he, like me, had a beach property—his was located in Ocean City, New Jersey. I shared a tad about my story and we both realized we had been on similar and timely journeys. This was interesting! I offered to send him, [1]*Come Away My Beloved*, a well-loved book by Frances J. Roberts, and Steven Curtis Chapman's CD, [2]"Beauty Will Rise." The CD was about the artist's heartfelt *Psalms* after tragically losing his adopted daughter. David said that he would send me some "propaganda" as well. All of my friends have learned to text with me, a necessity because of my busy schedule. When I asked David about texting,

I learned that he had only ever texted two times! Huh? Not a "techie"? We were having amazing fellowship. Two quarters of the way through this four-hour trip, I asked David if he was ever to marry again (following his impending divorce), what was he was hoping to find? (Just as if I was qualifying a client! Pray tell!) The words he then shared riveted me to the back of my seat. I was noticeably taken aback in disbelief! How could this man read my heart? How could he have extracted my unique expressions of words such as "woo," "treasure," or "cherish"? Feeling naked and exposed, all I could do was to hold my fist out for a fist bump with this stranger. I was intrigued. Near the end of the trip, headed into Atlanta where we would part ways, I grew quiet and contemplative. Curious if this could be a Divine connection, I deplaned and we exchanged a salutation. He was clearly not interested in a Florida property! I thought I may never see him again, but was moved and impressed. Exiting the gate, I found the information screen that would direct me to my next flight. Then here came Mr. Abel. Putting down his books and coat in a chair, and opening his arms up, he pulled me into a big bear hug embrace. What had happened? I know that whatever it was, was divinely holy. We exchanged goodbyes. As I walked through the vast terminals, I wondered if I might run into him again. Upon boarding my next flight home, I thought I would text this guy, come what may. My text read, *"It was very encouraging to meet a man of mission and character such as yourself."* He wrote me back immediately with nimble fingers: *"I am doing this just for you, and it is an honor. Ditto. Thank you. You were a healing balm to my heart. God bless, David."* Something happened on that plane. It was the beginning of a fairy tale and all who have learned of it have sensed the hand of God, the goose bumps of Divine intervention, and the unmistakable calling of two tattered, torn, and wholeheartedly surrendered souls to the God of their destiny.

Dreams

Throughout the years of my walk with God, He has always directed and revealed His will and future to me through His Word as revelation knowledge in my spirit. The stripping that God allowed, and the yearning He invoked, produced a sheer restlessness in me in regard to my future. Longing for the things I never experienced in a 35+ year-old marriage, the experiences of life I never knew because of my drive to succeed, and the intense desire to make a difference in God's Kingdom and "my world," I never knew what I was missing! Throughout the recent years of "shipwreck" and "upheaval," I have found a new "renaissance," a death of all I knew—good, mediocre, and stale changed to a renewed rebirth of anticipation, adventure, and *wonder*. The cloak of the old, tired heart had been removed and I realized that God's renovation of my heart had brought a resurrection of all I am. I had met my true soulmate on an airplane ride from California to Atlanta. Life, as I knew it, changed.

Following are texts I received from David during this time of change:

> *"With six billion people in the world, how is it that I met the one that is captivating my heart on an airplane ride to Atlanta? Thank you, Father. David."*
>
> *March 18, 2011*
>
> *"Heaven and earth touched on a plane ride to Atlanta. The Divine Author turned the page of a new chapter in my life. He enfleshed the desires of my heart. It is you, Tierney. Thank you, Father. David."*

Oasis

THE "PROPAGANDA" ARRIVED, as promised, and I was able to whet my appetite with pictures of my new friend's (MSF—"My Special Friend") home, fundraisers, beach house, CD's about Christian sexuality, books, and personally-scripted notebooks. I was overwhelmed at the quality of not only the print mediums, but the content of them. A personal, hand-written letter and regular phone calls into the night came with some engaging notes from David, asking for my opinions. He relished staying in touch. We spoke every night after 10:00, until at least 1:00 in the morning. This would happen at the end of our day when work was done and responsibilities were over. Together, we read aloud the book, [3] *The Five Love Languages: The Secret to Love That Lasts*, scripture passages, and excerpts of personal content as we had the opportunity, revealing the heart of each other from afar. We were comprehending the magnitude of our "meeting in the sky" as the multitude of daily texts and evening prayers occurred. What was God unfolding? We were both committed to God and family, highly successful in our careers, and had like minds on almost everything we talked about.

"Your good morning text melted my heart. I am so honored. Thank you! I will treasure your heart and protect it with all that I am. For this purpose, I have been called. I accept, Lord. It is my honor and privilege. David."

March 20, 2011

The honesty of our conversations penetrated past the initial membranes of our core beings. The pain of our purgings brought understanding and immediate camaraderie. David texted: *"The batteries of my heart are fully charged to overflowing. I have confidence in my step, clarity in my vision, determination to complete what God has put in my heart."* *March 13, 2011*

The texts were spontaneous and full of expression—they were speaking my love language! The 100th text came later and read:

"Four score and 99 texts ago, I had the honor and privilege of meeting a very beautiful woman who allowed me to open a very special place in my heart. She entered slowly and tenderly, bringing with her a healing peace, joy, and laughter I have not experienced in a long time. She is my very special friend whom I am learning to treasure in a very special way. Thank you for sharing the gift of this part of your life with me. Thank you also for allowing me inside your heart as your very special friend {YVSF}. David."

"One month and 327 texts ago, life as I had known it changed—a new springtime had begun. Life was emerging deep within me. Colors were more vibrant; laughter reverberated throughout my very soul. To what or to whom do I attribute this time of amazing GRACE in my life? It is my Heavenly Father that I offer all the thanksgiving, for it was He who entrusted His

most precious gift to me one month ago . . . YOU! YVSF {Your Very Special Friend}, David."

March 19, 2011

To David's admission, he had "no time" for adding a relationship in his life, but he had such peace when it came to me, and the expression resounded frequently. *"I don't understand it, but I'M ALL IN!"*

With both of our divorces in process but not yet finalized, we knew that this budding friendship may have to wait to define itself; however, the sparks were flying and the inward questions were abounding.

Due to the fact that David would have designated time with his children three weekends a month, he suggested that we try to get together once a month to provide an "oasis" for getting to know each other.

The first such invitation was one that included flying to Ocean City, New Jersey, one month after we first met. I flew into the Philadelphia Airport with butterflies in my stomach! I had never done anything like this before. I was flying to meet a man I had just met on an airplane and now I am going to stay at his historic "Princess Grace Kelly" beach house, as it was called, for a long weekend. I wasn't sure if I could remember what he looked like. I wondered, "What if there is no chemistry?" It was cold in March, and being a Florida girl, I was hoping for some beach time like I would have enjoyed at my beloved Palm Island Beach.

David was a true gentleman and prepared my "nest" with candles, chocolates, new sheets, robes, and slippers. His flair for flower arranging surfaced as he personally orchestrated a few bouquets. To top it off, he served coffee and fruit outside my door each morning.

It was cold and blustery. Indoor activity was the order of the weekend. It was supposed to snow. Oh, no! Between walking on the boardwalk, eating out, shopping in Cape May and Atlantic City, watching movies, and hysterically laughing and sharing, it was a perfect hacienda! At the beginning of the trip, I asked David what his goal for the weekend would be. He replied, "If I can grow to love you by the end of the weekend." I quipped, "You mean you don't already?"

> *"This weekend, I got to experience God's handiwork first-hand and it was exhilarating. It took my breath away. I was in wonder and awe at your beauty—seeing it first from a distance, then up close, then in the rapture of your embrace. I was in the Garden with the woman who was created by the Hand of God just for me! Thank you, Father. David." March 30, 2011*

Visit My Turf

THE NEXT MONTH brought plans for "MSF" to visit my turf. He would fly to my home and then we would drive to St. Augustine Beach for four days. An added bonus occurred when David found out that he could stay and visit throughout the entire weekend. We had a ball. We stopped at my office, went out to St. Armands Circle, visited two beaches, and rode bikes. The following day, we had pedicures and then vamoosed for a four-hour drive to St. Augustine Beach. We talked and compared notes incessantly. One of the highlights was when we stopped at two travel stores, Pilot and Love's, both clients of David's. There, he showed me an array of his products, inventions, and brands from his business, DAS Companies, Inc. His company was a grass roots start-up back in his youth that he pioneered with only $700, his father's station wagon, and his grandmother's garage. The company grew to be a $350M+ operation, providing electronics, antennas, lights, and thousands of other travel items manufactured in the U.S. and abroad for the travel industry. I marveled as I saw the depth of this man's commitment within his company's mission statement and the fact that 30% of their profits go to charity to support worldwide missions. My purpose in business, too, has always been to make a difference in the lives of others and present the gospel of hope and salvation to all.

David's Mission Statement:

DAS MISSION STATEMENT

To strive for excellence in all we do so that through our actions and examples we may be a model for others to follow.

CORE VALUES

DAS has seven core values through which the entire company is built. They are the foundation and essence of who we truly are to all we serve.

GOD HONORING — We are a stewardship company recognizing that everything we have is a gift from God. He entrusts the gift of His company to us, so that we may honor Him in all we endeavor to do.

FAMILY — Individual and corporate family go hand in hand as the building blocks of society and a company. Each must have at its core principals of trust, unity, respect, responsibility, balance and loyalty.

SERVANT LEADERSHIP — Every leader of our company bears the responsibility to nurture, grow and develop the potential growth of each and every associate they have the opportunity to lead. Associate's individual growth will be encouraged by the management team of DAS by means of training, recognition, communication, compassion and accountability.

INTEGRITY — The moral and ethical set of imprinted values of the heart can never be compromised in any decision of DAS. We must always have the courage to live them out through our corporate and personal actions.

HUMILITY — No one person is more important than another. DAS recognizes and values the importance of every associate's position, and how their contributions are an integral part of the overall success of the company.

QUALITY — We at DAS will always strive to attain the highest quality of service, products, marketing, communication and relationships.

PROFITABILITY — We have the responsibility to our associates, customers, suppliers, community and God, as managers of His company, to produce profits that enable us to reinvest for the future. This commitment helps us support and grow our associates, maximize our customer's profitability, and be an example of a stewardship company by sharing our profits with those in need around the world.

COMPANY PURPOSE

To build a profitable God-honoring business that through its actions and outreach will make a positive difference in the world which passes on from generation to generation.

Tierney's Mission Statement:

We had an incredibly etheric time in St. Augustine, touring the ancient sights and staying in rooms at an adorable bed and breakfast on the beach. One significant night was spent standing on tiptoes, kissing in the dark on St. Augustine Beach, watching the lightning storms, and then swinging in the two-person hammock for hours. What an enchanted evening! Returning to Bradenton, Florida, we attended church, ate out with friends, and then drove the convertible down to Palm Island. When we disembarked from the water taxi at Palm Island, we were greeted by a family who was celebrating the birthday of their 92-year-old mother. This dear lady came up to David and me, separately, touched our foreheads with oil, and blessed us! God was putting his fingerprint all over our times together.

Nightly phone calls continued and texts were the interlude of the days. Our next trip was fishing in St. Michaels! I flew to Baltimore and met David. This was a far different "reunion" than the first trip to Philly. The Cinderella story continued. We stayed at The Inn at Perry Cabin on the Chesapeake. We ate, laughed, and walked around the maritime museums, its lighthouses, and the waterways. We were always on a "top-secret" mission. Due to the nature of David's divorce, it was safest to remain in the wings, protecting the relationship. I called it a "wing-side" seat! We embarked to Tilghman Island to go fishing at Harrison House, a place where the men in the Abel family frequented as far back as 40 years ago. Captain Buddy was onboard his 55-foot boat, waiting for our trolling expedition. At the end of the morning of fishing, we caught 17 "keepers." The first catch of the day was my 32-inch striper—best catch of the day! We had a blast during that nostalgic trip where heaven and earth met, again.

Memories That Money Can't Buy

A S THE RELATIONSHIP exploded, I wanted my grown boys to meet the man in my life. My oldest son was in Hawaii completing DTS (Discipleship Training School) for Youth With A Mission (YWAM). My other son was in Los Angeles. Perfect! David asked if I would like to visit them because we felt that the consent from both boys in our relationship would be paramount. My oldest son was circumspect and, of course, his logical self. He said that he was excited to meet this "courter" and said that God is in the business of redeeming us for His service. My other son was more protective, but glad to hear that I was so happy. He wanted to do a thorough investigation of Mr. Abel! It was all set, so to Hawaii we went! It was a long trip, but oh, so worth it! The big island was not as scenic, with its lava foundations, as I thought it would be. We met up with my oldest son and had a special time eating and sightseeing, which included rubbing shoulders with Terry Bradshaw on a two-hour helicopter ride above the island. These were memories that money can't buy!

Regretfully, we left Hawaii, flew all night (of course, David slept the whole way), and we met up with my youngest son in the morning. We had a memorable time of eating, touring (The Getty's Museum, for one), and fellowshipping. We couldn't have had a better time of affirmation. My son said, "Mom, it's almost too good to be true, but it's everything I would have asked for you!" He later left me a "secret" note on my new iPad that said he was happy for me in this new season of life and that David took a load off of his heart and gave him hope for himself. Wow! Isn't that a beautiful by-product of what God does? I called David, "My Humble Giant (MHG)." I was amazed at his kindness, thoughtfulness, and generosity, not only to me, but to others. He often told me that I was "the script of his heart." "My love, this is one of the greatest awakenings of my life." "MHG" flew back to Pennsylvania the following day. I spent a fantastic day with my son before flying out the next morning. Mission accomplished!

Next Stop—Ireland

A MONTH LATER, WE were enroute to Ireland. David flew all the way to Florida to accompany me so I would not fly alone. (He spent all day in an airport, had four flight changes, and arrived at midnight.) Somebody pinch me!

Ireland was an exploration of six days which included over two days of ministry, supporting a ministry David had invested in. What a great trip! Spontaneity was the name of the game that included a different location, various bed and breakfasts, driving like maniacs on the wrong side of the road around hairpin turns, and slivering through roadways at high speeds.

The Trojan Horse

AFTER MONTHS OF hearing about David's property, businesses, and ministries, I had high hopes of visualizing, tasting, and seeing his world. Could I actually "slip in" to his signature event, a fundraiser, held at his home? It became a real life option as we arranged for my business partner and his "Indiana Jones" brother to attend. I would be their anonymous significant other. We still had to be careful not to unveil the dynamics of our relationship because all things in David's world were still resolving and he had been directed to protect our relationship. So I would arrive in the "Trojan Horse" incognito, with Paul and Bob as the vehicle. Paul and I flew into the Philadelphia Airport and met Bob. We were expected to go and stay at the home of Bob's friends who are dairy farmers in the area. We enjoyed their hospitality and slated our attendance for the *signature event* at David's estate for two nights. Everyone thought that I was either Paul's or Bob's wife. We saw David by day ever so carefully, and went to the events by night. It was so challenging to be on his grounds in the same location, but be forced to appear unfamiliar with each other. We passed the test. No one was suspicious at all. One of the sweetest events was meeting Mai-Lynn the first evening. She is David's beautiful daughter who

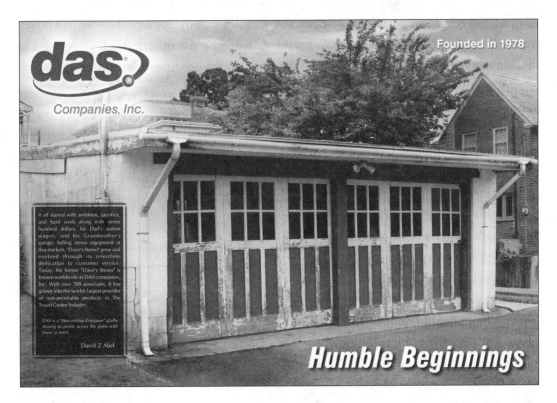

It all started with ambition, sacrifice, and hard work along with seven hundred dollars, his Dad's station wagon, and his Grandmother's garage. Selling stereo equipment at flea markets, "Dave's Stereo" grew and evolved through its relentless dedication to customer service. Today, the former "Dave's Stereo" is known worldwide as DAS companies, Inc. With over 700 associates, it has grown into the worlds largest provider of non-perishable products in The Travel Center Industry.

DAS is a "Stewardship Company" gladly sharing its profits across the globe with those in need.

David Z Abel

Founded in 1978

das Companies, Inc.

Humble Beginnings

has been an Abel for 16 years and is basically her daddy's caretaker, watching over the "chambers of his heart." She is an intuitive young woman who told me that she had never seen her daddy this happy in all her days. After the events, David and I took off and went to Tilghman Island and St. Michaels for a few days of rest and relaxation. While driving, we ventured through the town of Columbia, Pennsylvania where David grew up, and I saw the very antiquated garage where he started his homegrown business. We had a special time just "being," something neither of us got a chance to experience often. We fished and ate out, but spent a lot of quality time in reflection. I returned to Florida reluctantly, always sensing the Velcro pull upon parting. We came, we saw, we conquered!

Onward and Upward:
Palm Island, Florida

I WASN'T SURE HOW I would feel about returning to Palm Island; after all, I left my heart there when high property assessments and a depreciating real estate market caused me to give my villa to the bank. Being there with David added new significance, although it was very windy and the surf was wild. We stayed an extra day and played. It was a wonderful time of acting like kids, as evidenced by my riding on his back in the big pool, just hugging his neck. We loved being close.

Ocean City, New Jersey—Beach House, Here We Come!

WE STAYED AT the beach house for a week and frequented the Philadelphia Eagles' game. The seats were incredible as we watched from the 17th row behind the team at the 40-yard-line.

We made our way into New York City one day, a feat I had never experienced before. We had a bit of time before a matinee, so we walked around Times Square and tasted the sights and sounds of the "Big Apple." The day before I left, early in the morning, we had a narrow "escape" (you'll just have to be curious about that) and then drove to the commercial fishing pier on the Atlantic. Bluefish were migrating, as was I! A nasty sciatica nerve created distractions while riding bikes, fishing, or just hanging out at the "Princess Grace" beach house. David used skill and patience to land the biggest blue of the day. Using wooden rods that were over 35 years old from his fishing days with his father, he invited the big game to wear him down. As always, we gave away the "mess of fish" and enjoyed watching the happy recipients of the catch. No matter what we did, David found a way to gift others—mostly me!

As I write, I am sitting on a plane that is making an impromptu trip to Maryland where I can work on "our Harrison House" project. As always, I packed more than I would ever need. There is something about being prepared! Oh, and I have choices of what I can wear. I am anticipating a whirlwind trip, only to return home and pick up David and my youngest son in a few days.

"Script of My Heart"

H<small>E SAID,</small> "Y<small>OU</small> are the script of my heart . . . nothing less than everything I could want or would have asked for." Neither David nor I had ever heard that expression before. It was straight from the Heavenly Father, and even though it was coined as David's phrase, it was true about how I felt about him as well! He was the whole package, the whole "enchilada." He was a loving father, a successful businessman, a humble giver, and a romantic! I was overwhelmed and amazed that someone this perfectly matched for me could exist. More incredibly, was that on the heels of all my "wasteland" and "minefield of losses," this incredible gift of a man collided with my world. It seemed as if the convincing realization of this defined itself in the first two weeks of our friendship, as shown by our hundreds of texts and phone calls. God had quickly revealed that this was His Divine call on both of our lives. How unworthy I felt at times and how undone I was as I wrestled with the truth that someone could actually express such acceptance, love, and commitment to me. Over and over again, I would respond with my own insecurities and self-consciousness. How true it is that unless we are comfortable in our own skin, we do not know how to graciously receive true love.

This surprised me about myself because of my general self-assuredness and confidence. I guess it was because this was intimacy that was absent from my previous marriage. Believing in our own value and investment is crucial to steady and sure relationships. I must know and accept the intimacy of God, the Father, in order to be able to experience and give the same to another. Following previous rejections and abandonments, it is a treacherous path to stare at those fears in the face with the possibility of disappointment and disillusionment. I needed lots of affirmation and assurance for some reason. David is expressive, and his steady stream of verbal bouquets, along with his attentiveness, helped the insecurities melt away. For him, the deep chambers of his heart had always been untouched and unrealized. The mysterious ways of God allowed me to permeate the depth of his heart and bring a healing balm. I was oblivious to the ways God used my natural mannerisms and spirit to bind the wounds and see the Phoenix rising from the ashes. What sweet music we made together! We were melodious instruments in the hands of our Redeemer.

I reflected back four months before I met David, to a time when a pastor I had known, accompanied by a "prophet," stopped by my office when I was at my absolute bottom, emotionally. They did not know my trauma, but they prayed. The "prophet" told me that I was in transition and had been in "winter" when everything around looked like it was dormant, but spring was coming with new blossoms. Fruit was on the way. Romans 8:28 AMP applied, *We are assured and know that [God being a partner in their labor] all things work together and are [fitting into a plan] for good to and for those who love God and are called according to [His] design and purpose.* The "prophet" said it had to do with a strategy God had, a main relationship, validation, and my *dreams*. (Remember, God told me to dream, not merely hope, but rather to dream.)

Two weeks after we met, David's text to me read, *"I stood out on my balcony breathing in God's beauty, listening to His voice in the sounds of nature. They trumpeted in harmony—a new springtime is coming."*

March 13, 2011

When God speaks, He is not opposed to repeating himself, confirming His Word, and acknowledging His will. Spring had sprung!

Florida for a Few—The Waiting Room

D AVID FLEW IN for a short visit after his trip to Africa. He is so tenderhearted that it steals my heart again and again. When we embraced, he wiped away the tears. Our separations were difficult. We were in God's *Waiting Room*! Previously and individually, for both of us, we were in God's *Intensive Care Unit*. Both of us had similar journeys: losses, disappointments, personal hopelessness, and weariness from the battles, but our hearts were in tune with the Father. We were under His constant care as we mended and awaited healing. The Great Physician never left either of us, but the pain and trek was so intense that it seemed as though, He, too, had abandoned each of us. The yoke was so heavy and didn't seem to lift. I believed that it was better to have been moved to the *Waiting Room* together as God completed His work in and through us. To do that, lots of puzzle pieces had to be moved, but we sensed anticipation in our spirits.

My sons were both in town, so we were able to get together to make some special memories, including going to the movies, visiting Robinson Park, and yes, getting pedicures! Real men "do" pedicures! I have been so grateful that David has already "adopted" two more sons! He is playing an integral part in the healing of their hearts and the renewing of their minds. Yes, "it can be too good to be true" when it is the loving Hand of God.

James 1:17 AMP reads, *Every good gift and every perfect gift is from above; it comes down from the Father of all light, in Whom there can be no variation or shadow cast by His turning.* Proverbs 10: 22 AMP reads, *The blessing of the Lord—it makes rich, and He adds no sorrow with it.*

I texted David on June 13, 2011: *"Not long ago, we were in {God's} Emergency Room with separate issues yet similar journeys and symptoms! Today, we are in {God's} Waiting Room together. It is a much better place to be! I love you!"*

What Happens "In-Between?"

So God had spoken, but the timing isn't the same time you anticipated. What happens now? Fully engage! God is not done with all He has for you to accomplish and to learn. We are not just doing time, but rather, we are investing time. Two things last forever in God's economy: the unchangeable Word of God and people. God has "good works" for us to inspire in the hearts and lives of those with whom we rub shoulders. For some, broken relationships need to find forgiveness and release. For others, we are to be used to strengthen, support, and give counsel. You see, fairy tales are the pinnacle of our lives, but change, loss, and struggle is the daily diet in which we learn and grow. This is why so many of the scriptures address trials and tribulation. These, when responded to *with the grace of God, produce a harvest of right living, mature attitudes, and contagious joy*. The Word says that God will not allow the situation to become too hard for us, but will provide a way of escape *or* the wherewithal to go through it. Sometimes the best lessons are learned as we brave the battle and run to the roar. The stronger our will and resolve, the greater the preparation of our calling, and the more intense the trial will be. Ouch! For nearly four years of my life, the yoke continued to mount. I was being sucker-punched. Any one of the major situations in my life would have wreaked havoc in others. Why did my loving, Heavenly Father allow me to be pushed beyond my comprehension with losses, abandonments, and persecution? It was because of the great call in my future. Emptying self is not easy. People with control issues have a difficult time of letting go when they don't understand.

David and I continued to talk daily via the airways and meet through the airlines, at least monthly, if not more often. What an unbelievable storyline. As my father would have said, "Who'd a thunk?" Amidst David's 15 children, the care of my elderly mother, and our extreme business and ministry responsibilities, God continued to knit our hearts and paths. Each of us longed for the day when we would "do life" together.

Renaissance

WHEN MY FRIEND, Larry, learned of the dissolution and separation of my marriage, he wisely said, "You are ready for your renaissance now." All I had were questions after that statement. Two years later, he proved to be right. I had to go through the losses, the deaths, and the stripping of all things in order to have the rebirth and realization of the same. I came up with as many "R" words as I could. Perhaps you can add your own. These words expressed experiences that I was claiming for my life. One day, I would celebrate their understanding.

- ✦ Renaissance
- ✦ Resurrection
- ✦ Rebirth
- ✦ Reinvent
- ✦ Reignite

- Restore
- Reboot
- Rediscover
- Reorient
- Remobilize
- Rededicate
- Redesign
- Replace
- Refresh
- Revive
- Reinvigorate
- Rearrange
- Reenergize
- Restimulate
- Redo
- Reapply
- Resilience
- Rise from the Rubble

✦ Reconnect

✦ Release

I ended the list with *release* because that is what had to happen in order for *renaissance* to *begin*. I had to release my past husband from his humanity, failures, and omissions of the past 35+ years—almost my whole adult life! No broken relationships happen because of just one person. I had to *forgive myself* as much as anyone! Failure was not in my vocabulary. My tenacious nature did not understand the words "done," "enough," or "quit!" What would all those I had mentored over the years say? Was I giving the Kingdom of God a "black eye" by not sticking out the marriage? Had I done everything within my power to rectify and have a clear conscience upon his departure? I believe I had. Although divorce is not God's best plan, He does redeem us. Throughout the marriage, three-and-a-half-year separation, and divorce, I believe that I had acted in good conscience, always choosing the high road, always trusting God to meet my needs, and following His principles of integrity and preservation of the human spirit. In order to walk with my head up high and even to enter a new relationship without baggage, candid introspection must be done in the light of the Holy Spirit's search light.

I sometimes chuckle when I think of God and His omniscient plan as He orchestrated the meeting of David and me on that airplane ride from Anaheim to Atlanta. If either one of us had not experienced the Great Physician's surgical knife and had not been in the *Recovery Room* for a season, we would not have been ready for that foreordained plane ride which is merely a "plane fairy tale" today.

Out of the Ashes

URING THE WASTELAND of my life those three years, the silence was harrowing. I had too much quiet and I could not figure out why God had not changed my circumstances and rescued me. Proverbs 3:5-6 NKJV reads, . . . *lean not on your own understanding; In all your ways acknowledge Him, and He shall direct your paths.* Just what was He scripting? In that timeframe, I learned about the loss of Steven Curtis Chapman's adopted daughter and Chapman's personal CD of his own *Psalms* entitled, [4]"Beauty Will Rise." I had purchased the CD for myself and for some friends who had lost their newborn. While I talked to David on the airplane, learning of his losses, including his daughter, Brittany, I told him I would mail my CD to him. I later learned that it affected him in ways I had not figured. Along with him speaking to his trusted spiritual advisors after meeting me, and asking for confirmation, he also found the lyrics to offer promise, hope, and perhaps a future. Some of the lyrics to [5]"Beauty Will Rise" read:

> *But buried deep beneath all our broken dreams*
> *We have this hope*

Out of the ashes
Beauty will rise
And we will dance among the ruins
We will see it with our own eyes
Out of these ashes
Beauty will rise
For we know joy is coming
In the morning

In the morning
Beauty will rise

So take another breath for now
And let the tears come washing down
And if you can't believe
I will believe for you
'Cause I have seen the signs of spring
Just watch and see
In the morning,
I can hear it in the distance
And it's not too far away
It's the music
And the laughter of a wedding and a feast

I can almost feel the hand of God
Reaching for my face to wipe the tears away
You say "It's time to make everything new
Making it all new"

This is our hope
This is a promise
This is our hope
This is a promise

It will take our breath away
To see the beauty that's been made
Out of the ashes
Out of the ashes

These lines from Chapman's song not only ministered to David's heart, but to mine as well.

One-Year Anniversary Card

David, my Prince,

Take me away and let me rest on your shoulder and then let me kiss your lips with the passion I feel for you. You have disarmed my heart and my fears, bringing a constant ebb and flow of healing and wholeness to my weary soul. You have been a steady source of joy and encouragement every day for the past year. You have bandaged up the wounds, kissed them and held me, promising me a future and a hope.

I see my Father's hand and His love working through you, my knight. I am overwhelmed with your care and attentiveness. Thank you for your "yes" and for learning to text, sending email, and talking late into the night to grow and nourish our love and relationship.

"Love at first flight," a plane fairy tale—that's what our story is, a treasure chest of love, joy, healing, friendship, fellowship, and a future.

I love you with all I am.
Tierney

Disappointments Along
the Roller Coaster Ride

E VEN IN FAIRY tale romances, the ride can get bumpy and strewn with disappointments and delays . . . and more delays! There is no "normal" in the faith walk. Expectations must be lodged at the base of the cross where lives are submitted to our Heavenly Father and to each other. We bring our own baggage into our relationships and if Jesus is not the absolute center of our lives, and if we are not resigned to trusting in His will, a relationship cannot survive. With the boundary of logistics between David and me, his steady diet of Divine "interruptions," ministry, lending leadership at the helm of a megabusiness, 15 children, an impending and most difficult divorce and settlement, it was complicated. Add to this pile my constraints with running a demanding real estate business in a depressed market where my sustenance is based on not only hard work, but calculated endeavors, supporting a sizeable home, and being the primary caregiver to a failing, incapacitated mother. If our priorities were not aligned with God's, it could not work. The so called, "baggage," is not related to people, but rather it is related to responsibilities, habits, previous wounds, and fears of repeating past mistakes. God's fingerprints must be indelibly marked on the pathway to our destiny. The discipline of the Spirit-filled life must be our practice. We make hundreds of choices every day to do the right thing, to live and to speak honestly. Proverbs 18:21 AMP reads, *Death and life are in the power of the tongue.* The tongue can bless or curse, captivate or liberate, heal or hurt, defect or delight. Every day, we must shed the victim mentality, put on our "big girl" pants and take the risks that are offered in love. I John 4:18 AMP reads, . . . *perfect love casts out fear.* We must be givers, servants, encouragers, and be committed to pleasing our Audience of One. Ultimately, we account for ourselves. Thank God, He loves us in spite of ourselves.

So, my modern day Boaz (look in the Book of Ruth) is "all that!" Never losing sight of the fact that my real Provider is my Heavenly Father, He has chosen to favor me with the most amazing man I have ever known. Boaz was Ruth's provider, protector, and lover. The choices made by both Boaz and Ruth, before they met, were made because of their character and integrity. It was what made up the fabric of their union. Who we are the day before we say, "I do," is all we have to offer on the day after. We are a gift to each other—not our all in all, but rather, a token of who we have become. *We are His workmanship, created in Christ Jesus* (Ephesians 2:10 KJV). We are "a piece of work!" Thankfully, our Creator is not finished with us yet!

> *"Oh baby, there is no changing my mind, for my love for you is from the depths of my heart where God lives, not my head. I am responding to His music and invitation to court His daughter. David."*
>
> *July 13, 2011*

Analytical individuals want to know why. [6]"Enquiring minds want to know." When there is no explanation, no relief, no rescue, the real test unveils itself. In abandonment of my own security, understanding, and control, can I release myself to the One who has never given up on me? Will I fear the future? I John 4:18 TLB reads, *We need have no fear of someone who loves us perfectly; His perfect love for us eliminates all dread of what He might do to us. If we are afraid, it is for fear of what He might do to us and shows that we are not fully convinced that He really loves us.*

Childbirth is horrendous pain; however, when the baby is born, the pain is somehow forgotten. In retrospect, out of the fulfillment of "the promise," the character growth and lessons in suffering are worth the exchange.

How Much Patience Is Enough?

IT IS TIME! God works with a sundial! Me? I work with a stopwatch! I am a product of this society's expectation—be better, be faster, be the first, jump higher, dream bigger, and do it "yesterday." Although a year has passed rather quickly and rather laboriously at the same time, I never imagined God's timetable to be so detained. Dreams and visions of this long-distance relationship being "grounded" one day has come and gone. Landmarks of previous holidays and adventurous anniversaries have been eclipsed. Yet, our love is alive and in full bloom. David and I continue to see each other every three to four weeks, and converse and text throughout our daily schedules. However, there is an ache, a longing to be living life together, simultaneously, to not miss a thing. A long, arduous settlement has not come to completion as the very difficult details of divorce drags on for David. My situation seemed to languish on, but it was completed without anguish and suspicion—not David's! David, an astute businessman, has taken the baton and led even his attorney through the valleys of decision. His more than generous settlement terms have yet failed to thrust this event to conclusion. Months of anticipation have come and gone, but hope lives on. Perhaps it will be *this* week?

The waiting period should be the most eventful and engaging. For me, it is the most uncomfortable. I am the one who reads the last chapter first, who rushes past problems to solutions. I figured, I have already missed so much of the journey that I should not miss another moment. My conclusion is that once God reveals His will, we should embrace it and walk in it! Did He say enjoy the journey? Are there people and circumstances and a million moving gears in the cog of the wheel? Yes! So respectfully, I say, "Please hurry up!" My motto from several years past is, [7]"Tell me, what is it you plan to do with your one wild and precious life?" I missed phase one. I dare not miss anything else! Well! I/we have a lot of catching up to do! I am purposeful, a planner! I am not comfortable in oblivion! What about mom's arrangements, my business, my home, my real estate team and company, my friends? If I knew the timelines for David's and my "adventure" and union, I would be more effective in the now! Why is he so much more comfortable with all of this than I am? Is it because not that much will have to change for him? Yet, my Lord says in His Word (Job 23:10 AMP), *But He knows the way that I take [He has concern for it, appreciates, and pays attention to it]. When He has tried me, I shall come forth as refined gold [pure and luminous].* Lord, what if we run out of time? He says only, "Yes! I know!"

Psalm 31:15a AMP reads, *My times are in Your hands.* Psalm 121:8 AMP reads, *The Lord will keep your going out and your coming in from this time forth and forevermore.* Do I fail to see your plan? That even Jesus was in the place of preparation for 30 years in order to fulfill His calling in the three years that followed? Oh, Lord, say it isn't so! We have worked too hard, given too much, ministered unto weariness to *miss* "doing life together." I don't believe that either David or I could survive the pain of more loss. The soft voice of the Spirit comforted me and said, "My child, you have begun—you have read the last chapter. I am catching you up on the excerpts in between. *My grace is sufficient* (2 Corinthians 12:9 KJV)."

"For I know the plans I have for you, says the Lord, plans for well-being and not for trouble, to give you a future and a hope (Jeremiah 29:11 NLV). *The Lord will perfect that which concerns me* (Psalm 138:8 AMP). *All things work together* (Romans 8:28 KJV). All timing works together for those who love Me and are fitting into My plans. I am not moved by the second hand on your clock, nor am I unaware of the hour hand. You call Me Lord—then allow Me to be just that. You will see how well I do things—in My time, in My way because *My thoughts and ways are higher than yours.* You will, one day, see clearly My child. Move through this stage with trust and patience. I am about My Father's business of which you are a part."

Here, There, Or In the Air

WE TOOK A very quick trip to Ireland again for a meeting with the ministry there. I flew up earlier in the day because we would leave from Philadelphia at 9:00 that evening. David had a surprise for me! No, not a ring! We are engaged in our hearts with full-blown commitment, but due to the missing final divorce decree and the annulment process, which still looms, that will have to wait. I spent time in Elizabethtown, Pennsylvania, better known as "E-town," but always "under wraps." We drove around the property, surveyed the new barn and the blossoms, but with people yet around, and me being what I call David's "best kept secret," I haven't had the freedom to go inside the house on those visits. On this trip, however, everyone was told to take the afternoon off, and we had full reign of the house. It was so special to take time touring the rooms and refreshing my memory from the "Trojan Horse" experience one year ago. How time flies! We sat in the bedroom, stood on the balcony, watched a movie in the theatre, and then careened out the door for the airport. What a treat! We both cannot wait for this secret to be shared in E-town. It is imminent.

We flew to Dublin, Ireland, rented a car, and pretended to know where we were going on the wrong side of the road once again. We stayed one night at a lovely bed and breakfast and shared a wonderful meal in Glenborough. Our times together were precious and sweet. The next day, we went to church and saw the old Monastery Village, then left for Cavan, where the ministry is located. We spent leisure time enjoying the fact there were no time deadlines, curfews, or pressure. We both slept in and caught up with the time change. The following day was spent with the people at the Direction for Our Times (DFOT) ministry, consulting and planning. These are special people with a difficult call to the floundering country of Ireland that is in despair and financial drought. The people we saw at the airports and restaurants seemed empty and blank. They did not exude personality or embrace the light of the eye, the window of the soul. The ministry team there has an uphill climb as ambassadors for the Kingdom of God. Bless them, Lord! I picked up a few new Irish expressions: "no problem," "sure-sure," "ya-ya," and more! I even met a waitress whose first name was "Tierney," and another with "Tierney" as her last name!

We enjoyed being together on our rather grueling flights. Once back in Pennsylvania, we went to see David's mother, unannounced, mind you! She was charming and I was still in the holding pattern. It was really special to meet Frances and to love her amazing son on the sidelines. I checked into a "divey" hotel and was raised from my slumber by sirens and evacuation orders. Three times the blast penetrated my being. It was unnerving, and all for no reason, but rather a compromise in the security system. Aside from that, my curling iron was not working and the plane was leaving late. I jogged through the airport, but still missed my flights in Atlanta by minutes. I found myself placed in the first seat of the first class section, now wishing home wasn't so close! David and I had another incredible time together, only to say "goodbye" until another time. Soon, Lord! As he left me at the hotel, we said we would "see you here, there, or in the air."

I Say "Hello" and You Say "Goodbye"

Months earlier, I had slid into meeting David's mother in her room at the independent living center. At that time, she was chipper and physically able, but I was still "undercover." We had a nice visit, but it would be two months later that I would meet her again as David's "S.O. (Significant Other)." This time, she had been diagnosed with leukemia and was in an assisted living home in Lititz, Pennsylvania. She was failing fast and wanted to die. Still with all her wits about her, she allowed David and me to read, pray, and even sing a few Christmas carols with her. We visited her every day while I was in town. Her disparaging disposition only accelerated her desire to die. Mother Frances never lost her appetite or her faculties. David continued to see his mom every day and night. The day I left to go home, and two weeks before her death, David was sitting on her bed holding her hand. He told her that he loved her. She said it right back. As she sat there, she said, "David, I don't want to be bitter or angry anymore. I want the peace that you have." So David prayed with her, leading her in that prayer. She made sure he went slowly so she could pray every word with him, and she did. She hung on to every word as he led her in a prayer of repentance, known as the "Sinner's Prayer." Prior to that time, she was anxious and full of fear, knowing that ever since hospice was called in, her days were numbered. During that time of prayer, God also worked in David's life as a time of healing, forgiveness, and release.

Two weeks following, David asked me if I could fly up to Pennsylvania because he wanted me with him through the process. The well-known "death rattle" had begun its descent. Shortly after making those arrangements, Frances passed away. David had been with her in the morning when he talked to me, but then went home to take a nap. Brother Michael then called and said the end was imminent and he should come. Fifteen minutes before arriving at the nursing home, David spoke to his mother by phone and asked her to hold on until he got there, but she couldn't wait any longer. After her prayer, she experienced joy and peace. The enemy had let go and fear was dispelled. She had settled her account with her Heavenly Father.

A Beautiful Eulogy

After I arrived, we spent time with Brother Michael, his wife, Julie, the funeral home director, and the pastor who would be conducting the service. We then decided on the selections for Frances's service. After the service, there would be a gathering at the barn at Ironstone Ranch. Unresolved conflicts can keep us from many of the "would-be" blessings that God has for us. The service was beautiful and certainly a tribute to Frances. David shared a beautiful eulogy about her love for family, her commitment to the Lord, and her legacy.

Never Say Never

I ALWAYS BELIEVED THIS saying, but never to the degree that I profess it today. We must always remember that we are not our own. Did I ever believe that I would be the casualty of a divorce? Absolutely not! Wasn't it once proven to me that long-distance relationships never work? Of course, it was! How about 30 years earlier when I moved from the Midwest and sub-zero temperatures, to the sunny shores of Florida? Had I ever envisioned visiting "cold country" again, let alone moving to it? Remarry? Certainly, there would *never* be a man that could measure up to my expectations or the God-ordained disciplines I held in my life, let alone overcome the fears that would exist after a failed 30-something-year-old marriage. Then there is the *children factor*. I had raised two incredible young men. When I married, having children was void to me. I never thought about it. Now do this equation! David has 15 children, 12 of which are adopted from various and sundry countries—China, Vietnam, Albania, Haiti, Korea, and Thailand! Now add the complexity of his three birth children! What is the likelihood that they would welcome me into the fold? Coming from the past three years of a somewhat sedentary living (as I cared for my mom), to the home of diversity and activity, what was I thinking? All I know is that God said it, ordained it, and I love that man who I have appropriately called, "MHG (My Humble Giant)." Let's take the aspect of travel. We traveled at least once a month, hither and yon, never meeting anywhere for the first two years but in an airport. Me, the casual traveler? Me, living out of a suitcase? Me, the overachiever, over-packer, over-prepared? Say it isn't so! As I sit on yet another airplane to fly to Pennsylvania, where they are having an Arctic cold blast, it feels like second nature to have sprouted wings. So much for the eagle! That's me! I hardly recognize myself.

I just spent one week going through all of my clothes, jewelry, books, etc. I am a sinner—a sinner with Obsessive Compulsive Disorder (OCD) in this area. Somebody help me! I must have a different outfit for every day of the year! What am I doing leaving the salt, sun, and sand for a very different slice of heaven called, "Stone Gables Estate" and "Ironstone Ranch"? The most hilarious part of this dichotomy is that I actually packed cookbooks! Me, the athlete, the one who only concocted meals because I had to feed a family; me, who could never quite figure out why God chose to have us "waste" so much time on shopping, cooking, and cleaning. Holy smokes! Have I become a lunatic or a Pharisee? I remember they said that about Jesus, too. The truth is that I am a disciple. I am privileged to enter a whole new world of growth and stretching. Did I ever see myself "graduating" from my robust and fulfilling real estate career to begin all over again? It's like being born again—at this age!

The truth is that God has a sense of humor, and if we think we know the extent of His plan, we are fooling ourselves. His thoughts, His plans, and His ways are higher than ours. A helpless dependence on Him as He leads the way is our salvation and His delight.

What greater call could I embrace but to be in common-union (communion) with this most remarkable man, David Z. Abel? How incredible is the calling to be "life" to these beautiful children and to help inspire them to greatness? How privileged am I to be the "helpmate" and use my talents, gifts, experience, and heart to make an impact to the nations. As Luke 1:38 KJV reads, . . . *be it unto me according to Thy Word.*

We Did It, By Golly!

IT HAPPENED! GOD opened wide the gates and David and I embarked on our journey from Florida to Pennsylvania. He flew me up so I could drive down to my casa with him, gather my belongings, and "do life together." Ahhh, sweet! Finally!

The long Suburban was packed to the gills, with no room to spare—another David Abel adventure! (Do you know how many people have said to me that in aligning with him, I am in for an adventure?)

The 1860's farmhouse was fully under constructions and was to be the temporary dwelling for my mom and me. We wisely decided that it would be best to leave mom in familiar surroundings and warm climate until the frigid North thaws out. She is being kept by her committed caregiver of almost three years. God's provision totally amazes me.

With much left to do at the farmhouse, I stayed in the main house's apartment yet one more time while finishing touches were addressed. David and I teamed up and made satisfying design choices and furnishings for the quaint farmhouse which will be a bed and breakfast for brides and their bridal parties. With that in mind, we made it "Country-Elegant" or "Country Chic." It has been fun watching it materialize and seeing our mutual gifts complement and confirm our choices.

So, until the already seven-month annulment process is completed, I will live in and "fine-tune" the farmhouse bed and breakfast. How sweet it is to have choices!

While in Florida, we rendezvoused with David's older brother and his wife. How special it was as we ate at Anna Marie's Beach Bistro. The ironic thing is that upon moving to Florida 30 years earlier, I would walk down to this resort and go the beach twice a day—it was only three blocks from my mom and dad's home. God's plans are so incredible. What I know is that He redeems that which the *locust has eaten* (Joel 1:4 AMP), meaning: The loss of memories and significance can be "bought back" when the Holy Spirit is allowed to heal us and direct our paths. He is faithful.

Challenges with the Children

WALKING INTO A family of such diversity that is recovering from the disappointment of divorce is no small feat. The vast age differences and the role they each grasp for with their father cannot be taken lightly. I must find my place in the big *jigsaw puzzle* and still be me! My role is to support their dad, not replace their mom, and create a place of peace where they are free to be themselves and become the unique creations they were meant to be. God's grace is so complete, and His voice is discernible for every moment and each personality! We were even invited to dinner with David's eldest son and his wife! God's sweet healing balm is a-flowing, but what a ride!

The New Normal

Travel
Airports
Airplanes
Delayed Flights
Overweight Suitcases
Airport Food
People-Watching, Crying Babies
Stairs and More Stairs
New Friends
Lots of Traveling to Everywhere
New Nail Techs
New Hair Stylists
Smaller and Lighter Purses
Fast Pace
Company
Children/Schedules
More Prayer
Pasty Skin (Not!)

So what will the "new normal" be? I haven't the slightest idea, but "I'm ALL IN"—that is an "Abelism"—the instigator of activity, the organizer of schedule, I've had to be! From the days of teaching tennis when classes changed every hour and drills were held every ten minutes, to the regimen of real estate where appointments were protocol. Contracts had timelines, clients had limitations, and closings were always projected ahead with their thousands of details. Add to this mix a family, duties, ministry, other priorities, and friendships.

Flexibility is the new word. With freedom from the demands of the business day, because my career is now on the back burner, I am at David's mercy! Oh my! Or is it good grief? I am still adjusting my thinking only to realize that what was "normal" pressure, is not weighing on me. However, neither is a type of significance I have always known! Based on my identity with business, tennis, church, and friends, I am a "new me." I am meeting people who have no comprehension of my past, achievements, or talents. My phone is no longer my lifeline, nor is my computer my necessity. No, my iPad is always with me and I am a frequent visitor to social media sites! (Never say, never!) I'm okay with all of this! It must be the resident grace of God. After years of demand, non-stop phone use (or abuse!), and required schedule "lockdown," the fact that my phone is not lighting up (except for precious texts from David) and the emails are reduced to half, I'm really okay! In fact, I love it!

I am learning to enjoy the journey. I have joked that I am like apostle Paul who learned how to be content whether he had much or little and in whatever "state" he was in, *therewith to be content* (Philippians 4:11 KJV). So, whatever "state" I'm in (Florida, Pennsylvania, Maryland, New Jersey, California, etc.), I'm learning to be content. I say this after six-and-one-half hours of waiting in the Charlotte airport; the flight attendant has not made her way to the plane and we are already way overdue to board. My only rush is to see David after five days of visiting mom, friends, and doing business in Florida.

Wonder and Adventure

Hang on to your hat! This train is moving, usually a little tardy, but I get that. There are lots of people to get on board, and lots of details to wade through or deflect.

"Wonder" is when the man you love continues to "woo" you every day with the gift of himself. Whatever outward method he uses to do it, whether it's "sweet nothings," flowers, or just showing up grateful to the Father for His kindness, "I'm all in" with this amazing specimen of a true man, my lover, father, and hopefully soon . . . husband. (I say this as the annulment process rolls to the back side of the mountain.)

"Adventure" is every day. I loved real estate because of its diversity each day. Each situation was a new challenge, with new people and new demands on my expertise. That was only preparation for this next phase! Projects, trips, people, all are waiting for my nod. I think we are making up for lost time in this "new normal!"

Let's Get Serious! It's Not Either/Or, But Both/And . . .

FOR THE LAST 30+ years, I have been non-denominational, which means you rub shoulders and worship with people from all kinds of beliefs and religious backgrounds. I embrace expression of worship, music, dance, prayer in groups, messages that free-flow, and relationships. My beloved, David, is a deeply committed Catholic who believes the same things I do and he understands what his doctrines are. The ironic thing is that I love the believers in the Body of Christ, but I had a subtle attitude about Catholics. I hadn't met many like David who were passionate and alive in the Spirit. He put his convictions to work in supporting orphanages, missionaries, priests, and the needs of people, with the list going on and on. I had observed nominal Catholics who seemed to have a "form" of religion, but no power. They seemed to be in the performance cycles of attending Mass routinely and thinking that they earned salvation and favor by believing with their head and by doing things like ritualistic praying, kneeling, and communion. David's experience was different. His "Damascus Road Experience" was in the Catholic Church and it was real! The people he surrounded himself with were real—many young and genuine priests. His ministry efforts were embedded mostly inside the Catholic Church. I disdained "phony" or "pretense." I did not see "life" in all the kneeling, crossing your heart, sprinkled holy water, and communion where they actually believe that you eat and drink Jesus's body and blood. So, here I am, literally baptized, no, submerged in a Catholic world. David was quick to tell me that His calling was to be an instrument in uniting the One Body of Christ, to bring healing to it, and God has blessed him with the means to provide deep pockets of resources to do it.

Thankfully, David initiated taking me to an expressive full Gospel, non-denominational church called, "LCBC," a church model very much like my kindred church of Bayside Community Church in Florida. That was and is my life-line, my "life-support," my "like-kind." Not all of David's friends are Catholic, so they have welcomed me, but assuredly are amused about this love story founded in the heavenlies!

Just shoot me! I am in a strait betwixt two worlds! The "deepest waters" that left me speechless (yes, me!) and gasping for air was a two-hour Easter vigil, a once-a-year occurrence, and then a "High Mass" to dedicate a nun into the cloistered monastery. I was amidst sweetness, but also veiled heads kneeling up and down which seemed to be 20 or 30 times, and the whole ritualistic service was in Latin! Now, I took Latin in school, but this was not recognizable to me. It seemed like they could have gotten to the point quicker, easier, and in a more cognizant manner. Yet, these people are deeply committed to the pomp and ceremony. I couldn't find my way to the car and a nap quick enough. I believe in vivid expression, spontaneous worship, and illustrative messages. I would never try to "enlighten" David to "come on over to the other side," nor would he dream of pressuring me to adopt his Catholic doctrines. He has often declared that it is just like God to give him an Evangelical counterpart. Sometimes, I feel like a fish out of water or a second-class citizen while in a service or Mass. Then, David "levels" the playing field by worshipping and participating with me in my type of service.

I had an epiphany after the High Mass (High Stress), that our situation identifies David's calling to bring healing to the One Body. I told him that I was not trying to understand the routines, nor embrace them, but rather, to appreciate them and open up the hardness of my heart to what my mind closed down years ago.

That's it! It's okay to be in different "camps." We don't have to understand all the meanings or methods. We don't even have to agree, but we do have to appreciate each other. For the Body of Christ is made out of many different facets, beliefs, interpretations, and even denominations of people, but if Jesus Christ is the common denominator and His love binds us together, then the common fiber is to *appreciate* the truth. The fact is that He, Jesus, was born of a virgin, died, and was raised to life. His blood washes us from sin, and because of His great love, we can spend eternity with Him in Heaven. These are the anchors of our faith. These are the truths that connect our hearts and bring peace to our relationships. That which joins us together is greater than what separates us. How simply profound! So, I appreciate that it is not *either/or* but it is *both/and* as our faith is built upon the same cornerstone—Jesus Christ.

Detox

He wakens me in the morning.

In my "new normal," I have been awarded the luxury of sleep that I never appeared to need or want. So consumed by the draft of responsibility with family, a "rock star" business, and extended responsibilities, both inside and outside the home, I prided myself in the fact that I could get by on a "slight" sleep schedule. As a matter of fact, I could easily work 18 to 19 hours a day and be as sharp as ever. However, God is the giver of sleep. *He giveth His beloved sleep,* says the Psalms of David (Psalm 127:2 KJV). I claimed that truth for nursing moms, women with small children, or caregivers with loved ones who were ill. "Rest" and "sleep" were not equivocal in my mind's eye. However, if you are a Type A personality, driven, or an entrepreneurial spirit, you need both rest and sleep in order to be fully engaged and creative.

After moving to Ironstone Ranch and Stone Gables Estate, disembarking from my real estate career, maintaining a larger home, and juggling the details of the care of my aged, but spry, mother, I have slept in (at least until 6:30 to 7:00 a.m. on most days). Feeling guilty and less productive, I would voice my assessment to "MHG (My Humble Giant)." His support of my newfound practice and freedom has made me so very grateful. To take it even further, he has coined it as a temporary "detox" from the harried pace of the professional world and ranks. He is right. I'm disengaging from the drive to provide and achieve—from the "do-er" to the "be-er," from the "Martha" to the "Mary," from the pressure cooker to the shade of the fruit-bearer. God is resetting my base and transplanting my giftings. He is redirecting my pendulum. So often, we are resistant to that which is foreign or unfamiliar. Our security and our self-esteem come from what we have known, and parallels our experience. Sometimes, as we grow and change, the Holy Spirit whispers, "Get out of the boat." What? With no lifelines? No familiarity? No roots? No notoriety? No security blankets? And no "knowns"? Only the conviction of God, the Author and Finisher of our Faith, is at work girding our steps and setting our paths.

"She Will Wait For You"

A<small>RRIVING BACK FROM</small> the Ocean City beach house with the kids, there sat a letter from the Diocese of Harrisburg on the counter for David. He opened it up and wept! It was his release! The annulment papers had arrived. The letter took two months; however, the process took ten months. On the other hand, I had been notified that my decision had been made and was favorable, but it was sent to Philadelphia for ratification. It would be two weeks before my paperwork arrived (while we were in Florida at Disney with 18 members of the family). The annulment was never a "given." Had we not received affirmatives, we would not be married. The depth of the investigations and difficulty of the process did not lend itself to an automatic release of our past.

We took a trip to Ocean City with our daughter and her friends. While there, we got word that two of my friends had *Stage 4* cancer. David and I drove to a chapel to offer extended prayer for them. This happened to be the chapel where he took me upon rendezvousing the first month after we met. It was where God spoke to him and said, "She will wait for you." I recall thinking, 'Wait for you? How long of a time are we talking about?' We had no clue what that truly meant, but God, in His sovereignty completely understood. Why would God speak those words? Now I know.

Over two years later, as we were getting ready to leave the chapel, David took my hand and led me out of the pew into the center aisle. He knelt down on one knee and said, "Two years ago, in this place, God told me you would wait for me. Today, I am asking you to be my wife. Will you marry me?" Honestly, a fleeting thought I had as we drove to the church was that this could be a significant place where he could "pop the question." However, there were lots of those places; after all, we were on a mission to intercede for those precious friends.

Here he was, on his knee, in this chapel, with a few onlookers, sporting a ring and asking me to marry him. I think I said something cute like, "This is it? I'll have to think about it." Oh my! I am sure the delay gave him palpitations! Who could say "no" to this most amazing prince of a man? The ring is emblematic of his purity to me, his whole heartedness, and his commitment. It was lavish. It was certainly the most gorgeous representation I had seen. He imported the stone and had the supporting mount made to order.

One of my favorite sayings is that "God is in the business of importing and exporting!" God gave the green light, and we became engaged. How sweet it was to be able to talk about a wedding in the not-too-distant future. How splendid! While I thought I would be practical and get a versatile dress that I could wear for other events, I had some time to search while I was in Florida. No stores offered the "one" that said, "Pick me, pick me!" About a year ago, while getting my nails done, I was flipping through a bridal magazine. I saw "the" dress to dream of. I tore that page out of the magazine and tucked it away in a safe place. The day I went perusing stores, I went to the Something Blue bridal store. Casually and independently (what else?), I gazed at dresses. They carried the same brand name. Lo and behold, I pulled out a dress from their showroom supply (which usually means *available* and *cheaper*). Could this be the dress in my picture? It certainly resembles it, I thought. I tried it on and the people at the store said they could work with me, long distance, to perform any necessary alternations there would be! Is this just another expression of my Heavenly Father's intimate love and provision for me? I am so grateful for how personal He is and how His favor "chases me down." Perfect! This is just one more confirmation of this plane fairytale. I am so thankful!

"His"tory

THIS IS MY last flight from Sarasota, Florida to Pennsylvania before the wedding—with wedding dress in tow. Symbolism runs rampant because the wedding is on Friday, July 26, another anniversary, and 29 months after David and I met on an airplane. What a "blessed" tight rope it has been. The journey has been parallel to the gazelle leaping atop the rocks and cliffs, avoiding the crevasses, the pitfalls. I will be a bride adorned for her bridegroom, ready to celebrate the "love story," as Monsignor John Esseff puts it. In the first month of our courtship, he told David that I was his soulmate, brought into his life to bring healing. A month or so ago, he said he saw tremendous power in us in the quiet of the crest of the wave, before it breaks—a tsunami of power, he declared. For all that God has foreordained with this union, it is not unlikely for us to have had to hurdle over the physical and emotional obstacles, and believe me, we have encountered them! This is "His story" today—too much to detail. As the apostle Paul said, *I am bringing all of my energies to bear on this one thing; forgetting the past and looking forward to what lies ahead* (Philippians 3:13 TLB). Our worlds will never be the same! Our story still brings goose bumps to those who hear it, as the pungent exposure of our hearts is revealed. It is a story meant for the multitudes—the hopeless, the broken, the disillusioned, and those who have never tasted the Father's tender love for His children. The love that goes before us "imports and exports" the characters in our storylines, and the God who allows us to be broken heals us so we can embrace His Plan.

This journey has taken a boatload of trust, an ocean of faith, and a heart of peace. It truly is the likeness of the salvation experience up through the Resurrection! We meet the Master, we are swooned by His love, and we lay down everything we are and know, so His life can be resurrected in us. Marriage is the representation of God and the Church. The bride and bridegroom both have their respective roles, responsibilities, and privileges. The Wedding Feast will be when Christ comes for us and takes us to our new home (much like I will experience shortly as I move from my temporary spot in the farmhouse to the place prepared for me in the main house!).

> *David's text: "Baby, you are filling my heart with such anticipation! I'm a teenager, a bridegroom, a man whom God has chosen to entrust His most precious gift with—His daughter. Wow! I'm the most blessed man in the world! Love you, Dove!"*

BORA BORA IS PARADISE

There's a world of beauty to be discovered on the French Polynesian island of Bora Bora with its white sandy beaches and warm crystal clear waters.
The Intercontinental Resort Thalasso Spa Hotel, is situated in Motu Piti Aau, between the ocean and Bora Bora lagoon, with magnificent views all over the island and is only 20 minutes distance from the airport in private motorboat. The hotel has 80 private overwater villas of varying categories. The Thalassotherapy and Balneotherapy spa centers use water extracted from deep in the ocean for their treatments.

Oh, may the honeymoon never end! Speaking of honeymoon, let me tell you that ironic story, soon to become "His"tory! David is a very well-traveled man due to both his business and his mission work. He always wanted to go to Tahiti. When we spoke of a honeymoon, this was his dream. Before David (B.D.), while I was in the throes of all the destructions, it was suggested to me to have a dream board on my wall at work. So, I placed a few pictures of dear friends who brought joy to me and some pictures of beaches and water—my preoccupation! In a magazine, I saw a picture of the huts over the water. The little script called it, "Bora Bora." I never paid attention to that until a year or so ago when I asked my friend where Bora Bora was. He said that he thought it was in Tahiti.

It was not difficult to put two and two together! This is another confirmation of the craft of God implanting and creating the desires of our hearts. So, a honeymoon trip to Tahiti is in our not-so-distant future!

As you read this, it will all be history. As you celebrate with us, it will all be about "His"tory.

I am confident of this, that the one who began a good work in you will continue to complete it until the day of Christ Jesus (Philippians 1:6 NABRE).

May this book of *memoirs* light the fire of your spirit, warm your heart, and renew your love and trust in the God who has a future and a hope for each of us.

For I know well the plans I have in mind for you—oracle of the Lord—plans for your welfare and not for woe, so as to give you a future of hope (Jeremiah 29:11 NABRE).

My dearest Tierney,
        You are like the finest and rarest wine in the world which no amount of money can buy. This wine is a very special GIFT from the King to be treasured, tasted by all the sences, and savored by the chosen knight in His court. The beauty of the bouquet of this wine is to be shared with the world but tasted by just this one gallant warrior who has been tested in battle and who's loyality to the king is UNSHAKABLE. He alone has been entrusted with this rarest of rare vintages in His kingdom; the fruit of the grapes of His vineyard.
        A choice taste of this rare wine was offered to me ... All of my sences came alive as I inhaled the fragrance of the ever deepening beauty of its bouquet. They tingled and danced as if to the melodious sounds of a Heavenly song. My heart spilled forth poetry of love not written by the hand of man but by the "Finger of God."

Life free flowed from the very core of my masculinity.

I took the precious jewel encrusted crystal glass of your heart into my hands; gently, lovingly, softly, firmly, warmly. I cradled it, cherishing what had been entrusted to me, I inhaled an aroma that mere words can not describe. The fragrance penetrated every pore of my very being.

As I swirled the juices of the vessel, the memories of the times we had shared thus far were a symphony of colors and feelings erupting throughout my body. I had to sit down, my world was spinning. This experience was taking me into unknown, uncharted depths of Love that I never knew existed. I brought the crystal glass to my lips and tasted it for the first time. My palet was overwhelmed with the silky smooth richness, flavor and warmth. Every nook, crevice and opening in my mouth drank in its beauty. It felt like an angels wing gently stroked my lips. I wanted to savor the moment never wanting the experience to end. Around, and around, and around this rarest of vintages swirled until finially, with anticipation that curled my toes, I allowed it to flow down into the very depths of my soul.

    This was the first taste, of the first glass, of the finest, richest and rarest wine in the kings wine vault. It was entrusted to me as a life long keepsake from our king. I will cherish, protect, honor and drink from this most treasured gift from my king all the days of my life. As with all fine, rare wines they get richer, smoother, and more pleasurable to the palet as they age if stored and cared for in a very _safe_ place. I will store this gift of gifts in the inner sanctums of the vault of my heart where the tempature and conditions are just right for it to reach its fullest potential. It's bouquet will waft around the world causing it to be a much better place to hive.

Your Beloved
humble giant
xoxoxo

The Warrior

Prince Charming arrived one early morning on an airplane from Anaheim to Atlanta. Dressed as a casual wayfaring stranger, the purest of hearts was regally revealed. His Father had trained and "knighted" him divinely for His Kingdom Service. As he spoke to me, with his sword in its sheath, he unfolded the depth of his preparation amidst the Kingdom ruins. The skirmishes of battle were intensely threatening and dangerous to life and limb. His battle wounds were apparent, but had not sidelined this resilient warrior. His understanding of the Kingdom treasures were deep, and his use of the weapons were strategic and resourceful. He retraced story upon story of the attacks that were meant for his demise. This stalwart warrior refused to die. The wounds only intensified his determination to survive. Acutely recounting the lessons learned in the field, his Commission radiated his Position and his Purpose. He was now a force to be reckoned with—a Phoenix rising from the ashes of a final death blow.

The Father never left his side throughout the testing ground, and his older Brother interceded for his victory. The battle was vehement; however, the calling of Rank was greater still. This rare and determined Prince had now become a King, mighty in battle, tearing down the enemy's strongholds.

As is with all royal bloodlines, a sense of destiny lies within. This chivalrous leader has the undergirding of humility, gentleness, and dignity. He rules his kingdom with a sense of mercy and justice now. The threads of generosity stream through his cloak of righteousness.

I am honored to be in his court of maidens of which I have been chosen his handmaiden.

Tierney

PART II

Life Lessons Learned: His-Story

My Prelude

[8]"Every ending is just a new beginning that we fail to realize at the time." This line, from the movie, [9]*The Five People You Meet in Heaven*, gave me hope as my 30-year marriage was coming to an end. On Valentine's Day in 2009, I was asked to move out of my family home for the third time in four years. You see, four years earlier, I had an event that changed my life forever as my heart opened to the healing mercy and love of my Lord and Savior Jesus Christ. I confessed *all* of my sins for the first time in over 30 years to both God and my former spouse. The freedom and life I experienced, as God forgave me, set me free from a prison cell that had entombed me all of my adult life. When I shared this confession with my former spouse, it shattered her world and her heart.

At the time, I had 15 children. Twelve are adopted from around the world. Ten still lived at home. Now I found myself living in the apartment beneath the home we had built for my in-laws. Located just below the family home, these two rooms became my sanctuary, a place of great pain *and* healing. The great ache in my heart was almost debilitating at times as my mind swirled with thoughts of failure, abandonment, loss, guilt, and then came the "what if" cycle of the unknown. These are *all* tools used by the enemy of our souls, I came to learn. God, my Father, continued to send beautiful men and women into my life to speak truth into my heart, about *who* and *whose* I was. I am a child of God. He is my Father. I am a man created in the image and likeness of God. I am a father, a leader, a warrior, and a lover destined to share God's pure love. These were the truths that both my head and heart needed to hear. I learned to tune out the lies of the enemy.

'It was over. She had chosen to move on. I will wait for her,' were my thoughts. Lying in a fetal position and wailing late one night, the ache in my heart had become almost unbearable as tears of anguish, prayers, and groans from the depths of my soul arose from me to pierce the heart of God. That night I experienced a flood of His peace, His grace, and His love. He calmed me. I could almost feel Him cradling me in His arms because I was too weak to go on. Call it a vision, an inspiration, a dream, or a peek behind the curtain of my life's story about what God was going to allow me to experience: It was *hope*. God allowed me to see that I was going to court the heart of my beloved as a teenager, as a young man whom God had made "new again," pure, and chaste, experiencing *true love* the way it was meant to be. Overwhelmed and filled with hope and promise, my whole body tingled with anticipation, wondering how and when God would allow this to happen. There was light at the end of this deep dark tunnel of despair as I drifted off into a deep, peaceful, almost heavenly sleep. "Thank you, Father," were the words I uttered as I pondered about how this would ever be possible. "Trust in what God would do" was my resolve, although I did not know how this would ever come to pass.

A few days later, as I walked from my bedroom to the other room, I heard the still, quiet voice of God within my heart say, "David, if you walk this walk, it will become your story, and I will use it to help a multitude." In an instant, I knew the walk God was asking me to walk—one of a civil divorce and an annulment through the Catholic Church. Sitting down, I tried to process what this meant. 'How could I ever be divorced? How could I allow the children to go through this? What would everyone think?' These were all questions that raced through my mind. I wanted to shout out, "No! Not me!" Then I uttered the words, "Father, You know what is best for me, our children, and my former spouse. I surrender my will fully to Your will. Use me and my life's story for Your purpose."

My "yes" to the Father started me on a two-and-a-half-year journey of healing as a son of the Father, as a man, as a father, and as a husband-to-be. God used so many people to help me heal, to restore that which the enemy had tried to destroy. Meeting weekly with a small group of men in Chester, Pennsylvania every Friday morning helped in so many ways as I connected with what I call, a "Band of Brothers" in the Lord's army. Weekly, we would break open the "Bread of Life"—a Gospel reading from the Bible, and I would heal more and more each week as God's Word spoke truths to the inner sanctum of my soul. Every week, I started my two-hour drive for a one-hour meeting, then drove home two more hours and reflected. This time was both priceless and precious. Another group that God used in my healing process was a group of Christian CEO's called, "Convene," that met monthly in Lancaster, Pennsylvania, only about a 20-minute drive from my home. The wisdom that I gained there as a leader in the home, workplace, and the community, as we used the Bible as the textbook for leadership, again healed parts of me that God knew needed His healing balm.

Books were another tool that God used, as well as CD's of talks, especially related to my calling as a man. Gary Chapman's book, [10] *The Five Love Languages*, helped me understand my own top love languages and prepared me to speak the *love language* of another. Dr. Eggerichs' book, [11] *Love & Respect*, helped me understand what fills my heart as well as what fills the heart of another. It also revealed to me what empties hearts. A "God moment," as I call it, occurred one week when, on four different occasions, I heard people talk about the book, [12] *Wild at Heart*, written by John Eldredge. I thought it was odd that I heard about the same book four times in one week, but I am hard-headed at times and so I was not hearing God's voice being spoken through others. God's pet name for me is, "knuckle head," because it takes me three, four, five times, or more to finally "get it." I consider it a term of endearment, a pet name, delivered in *love* from my Father! The fifth time, God used my daughter, Hope, who had come to visit me in my apartment. A book fell off the shelf and she picked it up and said, "Daddy, I think you should read this book. I think it is important." "Look, daddy," she said as she handed it to me, "you highlighted parts you must have liked." The book was [13] *Wild at Heart* and the parts underlined were what I needed to read. God, my Father, wanted me, His son, to heal. Accidents, coincidences, odd moments, and strange occurrences are all just failures to see God at work. God was at work in a major way in my life. He is the Potter and we are the clay that He forms into His Masterpiece. Sometimes we need to be broken so that He can add His life-giving water to remold us on His wheel, in His hands into *what* and *who* He created us to be from the beginning: We become *a new creation* (2 Corinthians 5:17 NABRE) in Him when we fully surrender and give our all in "yes!"

The healing process is not a quick fix, but rather a long journey, as we let God into each and every chamber of our hearts. He is the ultimate physician of our hearts, minds, and bodies because He created each of us uniquely for both His delight and His purpose: to bring His love, Christ, into the world through the uniqueness of each and every one of us.

This brings us now to the beginning of our story, *Love at First Flight—a Plane Fairy Tale.* It is "His Story," or rather I mean to say, "My Story."

The Divine Appointment

THE CONVENE GROUP that I had been a part of for over four years was having its national convention in California. It was February, 2011, and I had decided not to go because I was in the throes of healing. I was alone and not open to a large gathering of happy couples. You see, the great yearning within me was to experience "true love," the promise I had been allowed to taste ever so briefly, ever so profoundly, a few years earlier. That feeling had grown as I patiently and obediently waited to see what the Lord would do. I knew I could never "date" because I believed it might reopen wounds in my heart, perhaps beyond repair. I was not open to a relationship, and ran at even the slightest overture from a woman. Then, at the January meeting of Convene, I realized that they had chosen me to receive the *National Award for Stewardship* at their February meeting. 'I do not want to go,' was my initial thought. However, I knew I could not let down all the people from around the country who had voted for me to receive this great honor. 'Ugh,' I thought. 'Okay. I will go to receive the award and fly home first thing in the morning of the following day.' "Book it, please," were the instructions I gave to my assistant.

Arriving the night before, I cocooned up in my single room passing up on the invitation from my friends to go out that night. The next day, I received the award, and again, with haste, made my exit back to the cocoon of my room. "Out of there, first thing in the morning," was my determined mission. Reading a good book or two on the flights home and then back into the sanctuary of my bedroom to curl up with God and cry was my plan, my agenda. But, you see, God had a different plan. I like to call it, "The Divine Appointment."

Early the next morning, I packed and caught a cab to the airport for an early morning flight. Excited about going home, climbing into bed, curling up under the covers, hugging my pillow, and sleeping were my top priorities. Before entering the plane, I always like to pray a little prayer that goes like this, "Father, allow me to sit where You want me to sit, share what You want me to share, and hear what You want me to hear. Please allow me to be a blessing to others on this flight."

As I made my way to my row on the plane, carrying the book I wanted to read, my heart sank when I realized that the seat that was booked for me was a middle seat. Ugh! Once again, I would have to endure bent and hurting knees, cramped arms, and a four-plus-hour trip. "Excuse me, young lady," I quipped. "May I take that seat?" She had piled her things on that seat, I had learned later, hoping that no one would sit there. After sitting down, she said, "You will get further if you call me 'Miss'." Oh my, radar up! That was a different response that put me on the alert. We made our introductions as the plane backed away from the terminal gate and then I continued to share with her for the next four hours about my "Damascus Road" story of addictions, acting out, brokenness, healing, restoration, and the whole "enchilada," leaving nothing out about my personal journey. "Do you mind if I ask another question?" was her polite way of learning more about my story. I felt totally safe, although I did not know why, to share with her the depths of my brokenness. She never judged me, but affirmed God's restoring love, forgiveness, and mercy as my story unfolded in great detail.

We both came to realize that we were on similar journeys of stripping the worldly things away and dealing with the loss of our previous spouses almost exactly two years earlier (mine on Valentine's Day and hers on Easter Day). Neither of us had ever dated during this period. We both were allowing God to heal us with our total dependency on Him. At some point in the journey, I expressed the importance of purity and chastity in my life and she asked the question, "Are you going to become a priest?" "No," was my immediate answer as I shared that I believed that was not God's vocation for my life. Then she asked the question, "So, if you were to ever marry again, what would it look like?" I pondered for only a moment, and then uttered words that pierced her heart, causing her to sit back in her seat with a gasp. I said, "I would want to woo, cherish, and treasure the heart of my beloved all the days of my life." Although I did not know it at the time, those were her words, the yearning of her heart to be wooed, cherished, and treasured by a man, a man the Lord had chosen, modeling how her Heavenly Father wooed, cherished, and treasured her.

A fist bump replaced words, disarming us both. We sat back to breathe. Something happened, and what it was we did not know.

"Do you text?" "Do you email?" The questions continued and my answer to both were, "no." "Let me show you how," was her response. "Okay." Not being computer literate and not interested in learning the computer or texting, I reluctantly agreed. Little did I know that this would be the tool that God would use in the beginning of *His Story of True Love*, the way it was meant to be. She shared snippets of her life with me throughout the four-hour flight, but her inquisitive mind kept probing ever so deeper into the intimacy of my wounds. Like the most skilled physician in open heart surgery, she entered into wounds that I had exposed to no one before. Rather than pain, God was using her as a "healing balm" to my heart.

The plane had landed and we gathered our belongings to get ready to exit. We both promised to send each other some items we believed that the Lord had put on our hearts, so we exchanged addresses. "Tierney" was her name, and she lived in Florida. She took care of her 93-year-old mother who lived with her, she was not Catholic, and we were parting ways. Oh, what was a Catholic boy to do? I was facing the final paperwork of my civil divorce, the final division of all assets, and the long unknown Catholic annulment process was ahead of me. "Goodbye," I said. Was it a final "farewell"? When I saw her looking at the flight board, I walked over, put down my bags, opened my coat, and gave her a parting hug. Off to our flights we went.

The flight we were on was a Delta flight. "Delta" means, "new beginnings." "What was God up to?" I pondered. Words from a friend, spoken to me the day before my California flight, kept echoing in my head. He said, "You need to be open to receive the woman that God is going to bring into your life."

A Healing Balm to My Heart

Settling into my seat on my final flight home, my phone buzzed. I had received a text, a text message from Tierney. It read:

> February 26:
> *"Just for the fun of it . . . a text! It was very encouraging to meet a man of mission and character as yourself. God bless, Tierney."*

I responded:

> *"I am doing this just for you, and it is an honor. Ditto. Thank you. You were a healing balm to my heart. God bless, David."*

As I reflected on the next flight home, I could not help but wonder, "What was God was up to?" I shared my *whole* story, from brokenness and my addictions, to God's work in my life -- and she did not run or look for a parachute with which to jump out. Rather, she wanted to learn more. Sharing what was happening in her daily life and asking about my day became the norm every night, starting at about 10:30 and continuing until 1:00 or 2:00 in the morning. During these hours and hours of sharing by text and phone calls into the wee hours of the morning each night was not only growing our friendship, but was also allowing us to experience God's unconditional love through each other. We had come to ache with anticipation for the text or call so we could share with each other. Unknown to Tierney at the time, I would take a nap from 8:30 to 10:30 p.m., setting my phone alarm, so that I would be alert and interactive with my "special friend."

Almost from the very beginning, our friendship grew into a courtship. My heart raced with eager anticipation for a text or call from her. Healing was occurring in parts of my heart as the balm of her very essence, ever so gently, ever so lovingly, entered through the very wounds that once were portals of pain. After two weeks, I knew something much more than a special friendship was developing. Love poetry, like the "Song of Songs," was flowing from my heart like I had never experienced before. It was as if Christ was wooing the heart of His beloved through me. He was the One courting His beloved with Divine words that pierced the very core (heart) of Tierney, causing moments of heavenly ecstasy deep within her, so pure that both of us could not truly put into words what was happening. The "Divine Lover," you see, was courting both of us purely and chastely through the other. It was and still is a heavenly dance with our Bridegroom, Christ, through the humanity of each of us. God demonstrates His love to each of us through the other as His son and daughter, His brother and sister, and His bride.

> My March 13, 2011 text message to Tierney read:
>
> *"My batteries of my heart are fully charged to overflowing. I have confidence in my step, clarity in my vision, determination to complete what God has put in my heart. Thanks so much for your special and treasured wind in my sails. Your feathers are growing back. I would be honored to be the wind beneath your wings to take you to the highest heights. God has great plans for you. He has been preparing you for His purpose. Thanks for sharing your heart with me."*

Obedience

I KNEW THAT I needed to share what was happening in my heart with my inner circle of three to hear their discernment and counsel. Knowing that I must first and foremost honor God in this relationship/courtship, I needed the spiritual guidance of those He had put in my life: Monsignor John Esseff, my spiritual director who was also Mother Teresa's spiritual director for many years (his spiritual director was St. Padre Pio), Anne, a lay Apostle from Direction for Our Times (DFOT), and Euse Mita, my bookend brother in Christ. The first call went out to Anne in Ireland.

Three years earlier, Anne had prayed with me in the Adoration Chapel and the Lord had revealed to her deep truths about my life's journey. What I remembered most vividly was that during her prayer, with her hand on my back the entire 40 minutes, I felt something like an electric pulse course through my body, almost like a heartbeat. It was as if she was entering into the very core of my heart. No words were spoken during this entire time, but after about 20 minutes, she let out an audible gasp and my tear ducts opened up like floodgates as I wept. When the 40 minutes of prayer time ended, she sat in front of me and shared God's deep love for me. I journaled seven pages of what she revealed. The part that I can never forget is that during the deep prayer time, two saints appeared in a vision to Anne. They were St. Joseph and St. Padre Pio, both with sad faces. In Anne's deep contemplative prayer vision, she asked them why they had sad faces. "Was it because of this man's sins?" Anne asked in prayer. St. Joseph answered, "No. It is because of the deep wounding of this man's heart." Anne continued to share with me so many truths. God had allowed her the opportunity to be the conduit of His love, His truths, and His message of hope and healing.

As I shared my story and what I was experiencing in my heart, the joy, delight, and excitement that Anne shared with me about what God was both bringing and allowing in my life, caused me to break down and weep with a depth of feelings that I had not experienced, perhaps ever before. Hope, promise, redemption, resurrection, compassion, mercy, healing, and true love, as it was meant to be from the beginning, was the essence of the message she shared.

When I hung up the phone, I felt like a teenage boy. Euphoria, the light of hope at the end of this dark tunnel that I had been in for so many years, was warming me all over as my whole body tingled with excitement. Obedience to God and His Church was the walk I knew I needed to walk in total surrender to God's will of what was going on within me. The first confirmation was Anne; the second was revealed through my Spiritual Director in Scranton, Pennsylvania, Monsignor John Esseff. When I arrived, he greeted me with such enthusiasm and joy, as if God the Father was embracing me and celebrating with me what He was doing for His son. I could hardly wait to share. Each step I made toward his room was one step closer to the wellspring of joy that was to burst forth from my heart. He sat back in his recliner, closed his eyes, folded his hands, and said, "Let's pray, David, and give glory to God for what He is doing in your life." When his prayer was finished, I felt as if I was enveloped in God the Father's love, and was in total peace. "Share what God is doing in your life, David," was all he said, and the floodgates of my heart broke loose in the story of the "Dance of Love," that I was experiencing. His eyes remained closed, but the grin on his face kept getting broader and broader. When I finally took a breath about 30 minutes later, he sat up in his chair with a face and smile that was so radiant, so filled with joy, and beaming with heavenly delight. He then spoke these words: "David, you need to receive the gift. God has brought her into your life to heal parts of your heart that I cannot touch. She is your soul mate and she will be your wife. You need to complete the annulment process as rapidly as possible, without delay." I think I slumped back into my chair and my bottom jaw bounced off the floor. What I was looking for was confirmation of what God was doing with a total willingness to surrender to His will in what was happening in my life in full obedience to Christ and His Church. What I got was "Divine Prophecy" about what was to come to pass two-and-a-half years later. The other counsel he gave was exactly the counsel that Anne had given me to the exact word. "David, you must protect this relationship. You must not share it with anyone outside your inner circle. You must defend the heart of your beloved."

"Wow!" I had not even taken Tierney out for the first time; however, in some way, I knew that what both had spoken to me was not only in harmony with each other, but with what God was revealing in my heart. The third call I made was to my best friend, Euse Mita. As I shared the story with him, I could almost feel his love and approval. He said, "David, you know I am dead set against divorce because I come from a broken home and am a product of it; however, knowing your story and your journey as intimately as I do gives me *great hope* in what God is doing for my brother. David, receive the *gift*.

Experience *true love* the way it was meant to be and, oh, by the way, when do I get to meet her? She must be some kind of woman." I told him she was flying to Philly the next week and this would be the first time I was going to see her since the plane ride. Euse said, "Bring her by the office, bro, I really want to meet her." "You got it," I said. "We will see you right after I pick her up from the airport." The plans were made; I received three confirmations from the Lord, from my accountability/spiritual direction and protection team. It was unanimous that God was at work.

My March 16, 2011 text message to Tierney read:

"With all my heart, I want to see your face, gaze endlessly into your eyes, and just snuggle into the captivating beauty of your heart!"

My March 19, 2011 text message to Tierney read:

"One month and 327 texts ago, life as I had known it changed . . . a new springtime had begun . . . life was emerging deep within me. Colors were more vibrant; laughter reverberated throughout my very soul. To what or to whom do I attribute this time of amazing GRACE in my life? It is to my heavenly Father that I offer all the thanksgiving, for it was He who entrusted His most precious gift to me one month ago . . . YOU! YVSF {Your Very Special Friend}"

My March 20, 2011 text message to Tierney read:

"Wow! You are sending me Divine heavenly kisses this morning. You are wooing my heart in a very tender, special way. Thank you, Father, for allowing me to trust Tierney with the key to that very special place in my heart. I feel so protected in her tender hands. She, Father, is a GIFT beyond my dreams. Thank you so much again, Father!"

First Date

To say I was like a teenage boy, with butterflies in my stomach and a bounce in my step, was an understatement. Everything had to be perfect. I had invited Tierney to fly to Philadelphia, go to see my best friend, Euse, and then visit my beach house in Ocean City, New Jersey. She had accepted!

Texts throughout the day, telephone calls, and of course, our nightly sharing sessions continued with great anticipation as well as wonder. What was the Lord up to? When Tierney read to me from the Bible every night about what the Lord had put on her heart, it set my heart ablaze. I had never experienced this before and would highly recommend it to all couples because God's Word continued to bathe me with His ointment of love. Hearing God's heart in His Words, coming from the heart of my beloved Tierney, captivated me. I ached and yearned so deeply every night for more.

The day had finally arrived! My Dove, my beloved, was flying into the Philadelphia International Airport, only 30 days after we first met. Our first date was going to happen! Oh, my! I felt like a teenager. The vision God had allowed me to taste, deep within the recesses of my heart two years earlier, was happening. Every fiber and nerve ending in my body was tingling with breathless excitement. This was so different for me because, you see, it was the purification of both my mind and body from sexual addiction and pornography that set me free to experience the true beauty of the "Dance of Love" within me. It was not lust that drove me, but the rocket fuel of purity and chastity that ignited in me a deep desire to win the heart of my beloved, Tierney. God, the Father, was choosing me to purely love His daughter, His sister, and His bride through me. Lust is like drinking saltwater, thinking it will quench your thirst. It does the opposite. It kills you. Drinking the living waters of God from the vessel He has chosen for you is like experiencing God's love for you, flowing through a purified vessel, and that vessel God chose for me was and is Tierney.

I had no fear of falling, sexually, with Tierney. From the beginning, I had shared with her the absolute importance of purity and chastity in my journey. She rejoiced in my position because it was absolutely her heart's desire, too. I remember her text response, and again it was a confirmation of God's hand in the story of our journey. *"I will protect and guard your purity and chastity, David,"* were the words she texted—music to my very soul.

I drove to the beach house the day before her arrival to prepare her nest—the room in which she would be staying. New sheets, two bathrobes, two pairs of slippers, two bunches of flowers that I personally arranged in her favorite colors, vanilla-scented candles (her favorite), and other provisions accompanied me to the beach house. I sang and almost floated as I went from room to room. I wanted to make sure everything was just perfect. The master bedroom, with the fire burning in the fireplace and views of the ocean from the bed, would be her room for the three-day weekend. I would sleep in the room across the hall. I could hardly sleep at all the night before. Prayers, prayers, and more prayers to the Father kept pouring out of me. I wanted so much to honor Him by honoring His daughter.

As I drove to the airport the next morning, I just kept listening to the songs from the CD that Tierney had sent to me after we first met. It was entitled, [14]"Beauty will Rise," by Steven Curtis Chapman, and the songs on it were my story. They ministered to me, filling me with peace, joy, and a sense of such a great hope in what God was doing. I remembered the items I had sent to Tierney the next day after we had met and chuckled. The four-CD set by my friend, Christopher West, entitled, [15]*Theology of the Body*, was all about purity, chastity, and marriage—the way God had intended it to be from the beginning. Tierney and I were going to live out what the Bible teaches about why God created us male and female—the way it was meant to be "in the Garden."

I made my way to the luggage belt at the Philadelphia Airport, scanning all the people in my search for Tierney. There she was, with cell phone in hand and texting, "Where are you?" As I approached her, our eyes met and our faces beamed. I wrapped her in a hug and whispered in her ear, "It is so good to see you again. Thank you so much for coming." I remembered on my drive to Philadelphia and the whole day before that my greatest longing was to hold her hand. As we crossed the road to my car with luggage in tow, she slipped her hand into mine ever so tenderly. I felt shock waves pulse through my body, my knees became weak, and my toes curled as tears welled up in my eyes. I believe my very soul was crying healing tears of joy.

We loaded luggage into the car and headed down Route 95 toward the office of my friend, Euse Mita, in Chester, Pennsylvania. About half-way there, my cell phone rang. It was Euse, so I took the call. He screamed through the telephone that his son was having a brain seizure while driving and asked that I pray for him because his son was almost killed. I turned pale. What if his son's brain tumor was returning after three years of remission? My heart ached in pain for my friend as he faced this battle again for his son. Plans had changed, and Tierney and I could not go to meet him. I shared what had just happened with Tierney and asked her if it was okay if we went somewhere else before the beach house so that we could pray for Euse's son. She readily agreed and we made our way to a Catholic Church in Linwood, New Jersey that has Eucharist Adoration. We entered the church, went into the pew, and prayed on our knees side-by-side for almost two hours. I remember such a sense of unity in our spirits as we were joined together, kneeling in prayer to God at that Catholic Church.

There was oneness in purpose and heart. No words were spoken the entire time; however, when we left the church, Tierney asked me, "Did the Lord speak to you?" "Yes," I answered. "What did He say," she continued. "Do you want to know?" I asked. "Yes, I do." Her inquisitive heart wanted to know what the Lord had spoken to me. I told Tierney that the Lord said, "She will wait for you." No more questions followed as we both pondered what the Lord had spoken to me. Tierney did wait two-and-a-half years for me until we were joined as husband and wife in a Sacramental Marriage in the Catholic Church.

We arrived at the beach house and I showed my Dove (my pet name for Tierney as I invited her into the nest of my heart) the house and her room. Later, we went to dinner and enjoyed my favorite meal, Hawaiian grouper, at the Anchorage in Somers Point. Romance was in the air as we shared and shared and shared our life stories. Back in the house, sitting by the fireplace in the living room and watching a movie, brought to a close our first night as we retired to our bedrooms, hardly able to sleep as we recounted all that we had shared and experienced. I fell asleep, praising God for the gift of his most precious daughter, Tierney, and the healing that she was (and is) to my heart.

In the morning, I prepared a breakfast tray for Tierney and sat it outside the door to her room. Then I went out to my car and prepared to drive to morning Mass. As I was getting in the car, I looked up to see her on the balcony. She was almost entranced as she watched waves crash on the beach. I later learned that she was worshipping God and giving thanks for all He was doing. "Breakfast is outside your door. I'm going to Mass—be back shortly!" I called up. During the entire trip to Mass, I kept thanking God for Tierney and asking Him to help me court her purely. During Mass, my heart exploded in worship and emotion as I wept with tears of joy that washed over me.

Throughout the day, we enjoyed riding bikes on the boardwalk, strolling for miles along the beach hand-in-hand, and tender embraces. Then came our first kiss. Oh, my! The word I would use to describe our lips touching for the first time would be, *electrifying*. Tierney always likes to ask questions, and so she posed this question to me: "What's the one thing you would like to accomplish in our time together this weekend?" Without a moment's hesitation, I responded, "I would like to fall in love with you." "What? You mean you haven't already?" she quipped in reply, to which we both laughed as I wrapped my arms around her and held her close.

On the last morning of our time together that weekend, we held each other close on a double chaise lounge that was situated on the porch of the beach house overlooking the ocean. As I peered deeply into Tierney's eyes, I spoke these words from my heart, "I love you." Our first date was coming to an end, but in reality, it was merely the closing of the first chapter of the book that God was writing of our lives together.

Memories that money cannot buy were created over that long weekend in Ocean City, New Jersey. As I gazed into the eyes of my beloved Tierney at Sunset Beach in Cape May, God painted an eruption of colors on the canvas of His cloud-swept sky. The final rays of the setting sun glistened and moved to the sound of the crashing waves on the beach where we stood. We strolled along the boardwalk hand-in-hand, breathing in what God was doing in our hearts. We then tucked away in a sheltered nook by the Wonderland Pier to snuggle in each other's arms, and I experienced once again the true wonder and beauty of my beloved's kiss. A glass of wine in front of the fireplace, and endless sharing of our life stories, was like starbursts of joy and wonder, knowing that God was at work in the continuing story of our lives.

My March 30, 2011 text message to Tierney read:

"This weekend, I got to experience God's handiwork first-hand and it was exhilarating. It took my breath away. I was in wonder and awe at your beauty—seeing it first from a distance, then up close, then in the rapture of your embrace. I was in the Garden with the woman who was created by the Hand of God just for me! Thank you, Father. David."

My March 31, 2011 text message to Tierney read:

"Heaven and earth touched on a plane ride to Atlanta. The Divine Author turned the page of a new chapter in my life. He enfleshed the desires of my heart. It is you, Tierney. Thank you, Father. David."

Another March 30, 2011 text message to Tierney read:

"Good morning, my Dove! The cool, refreshing waters of the wellspring of my HEART await you. Whenever you need to refresh, renew, and quench your thirst, come to the life-giving waters of my heart. It is your private oasis. Bathe in its waters—they are yours. Your Beloved. David."

Tierney's Turf, Florida

WHEN WE PARTED at the airport, Tierney and I agreed that we would get together once a month for a long weekend. Our next meeting place would be in Tierney's, dare I say, beloved Florida. I was like a teenage boy when I arrived back home, and this feeling continued throughout the month. Love poetry poured out of my heart to Tierney almost every day. My body would tingle with excitement when she would text or call. It was like nothing I had experienced before. The next week, I was back in church at Adoration, pouring out my heart to the Lord, thanking Him over and over again for His gift of gifts to me. I vividly remember once during this time of prayer and worship, just after I had thanked Jesus for the gift of Tierney in my life, I heard in my heart, "My Mother chose her for you." I had no doubt when I heard this that Mother Mary had chosen Tierney for me. It was then that I came to understand that Tierney was and is the '*Script of my Heart.*' Scripted by God from the beginning and penned deep into the core of my heart was our story—the way it was meant to be from the beginning.

Thirty days went by quickly, and soon I arrived at the Sarasota/Bradenton airport. There she was, beaming with beauty and radiating a joy that pierced my heart as I wrapped her in my arms. I remember thinking, 'I never want to let go. I just wanted her to stay in my arms and dance.' We made our way to her car with an occasional stop along the way just to hold each other, exchanging, without words, our gratitude to the Father and each other. Holding hands was our favorite thing to do, along with sharing our life stories. Tierney, from the very beginning, loved to read from the Bible to me. She would say, "The Lord put this verse on my heart for you, David." She would read it and it was exactly what I needed to hear. It was as if God, the Father, was using His daughter to speak His healing words of affirmation into my heart. Tierney was the vessel God was using to allow me to drink living water from His well of truth. Redemption, resurrection, and renewal were all occurring within me. A Phoenix rising from the ashes was the visual picture Tierney shared with me on our way to her home. It resonated so true. I was becoming the man God had created me to be from the beginning, courting the heart of my beloved. It felt as though I was "back in the Garden of Eden," pure and innocent, because I believe I was and am a new creation in Christ.

We arrived at Tierney's beautiful home that was nestled in what looked like a garden paradise along a meandering creek. *Paradise*, in an earthly way, would be the word I would use to describe it. The interior of the home popped with colors and life, expressing outwardly what was Tierney's inner eye for beauty. Situated off the back was a rock-shaped pool with a hot tub and a plethora of tropical plants, both inside the screen-enclosed pool and continuing as far as I could see. The final room Tierney showed me in her house contained her most precious occupant—her 93-year-old mother, Pat, who lived with her. Her mother lit up as we walked in the room and I saw immediately where Tierney got her beauty from.

Oh, my! The similarities abounded as we sat on the edge of Pat's bed and I shared the story of my life with her. She had such a deep and intimate relationship with God that radiated through both her words as well as her smile which lit up, not only the room, but every heart in it.

Tierney's mom commented to Tierney as we parted on our way to St. Augustine, "He's a keeper. He's relative material." She did not mince words. Her heart spoke the truth to me of what she was experiencing in our short time together: "She approves of you, David." Once again, God's confirmation came. We were walking out His story.

> On April 17, 2011, Tierney texted this message: *"My mom just said something that surprised me. She said, 'I love his voice!' I asked, 'Why?' and she said, 'I don't know – just something about it.'"*

That night in my bedroom at Tierney's home, the Father spoke these words to my heart:

> "*Trust in the Lord with all your hearts*, David and Tierney. *Rely not on all your ways. Be mindful of Him and He will make straight your paths.* You both do not fully understand what I am doing, but I am asking you both to <u>trust Me</u> and rely not on the way you would normally think. Honor Me is all both of you need to do and I will take the bumps and curves out of what looks like an impossible journey. *Honor the Lord with your wealth, with first fruits of all your produce* (Proverbs 3:9 NABRE). I am speaking of all the gifts, talents, worldly goods, and everything I have entrusted with you to use to bring Me honor and glory."

"By doing this, your barn (soul) will be filled with grain (the Bread of Life, My Son) and New Wine (My Son, Jesus), and your vat (heart) will overflow. My son (and daughter), distain not the discipline of the Lord. Spurn not His reproof. I want to grow both of you in holiness and it will require you both to be willing to learn, to be stretched, to change. *Your ways are not My ways—be open to My ways."*

"For whom the Lord loves, He reproves and He chastises the son (and daughter) He favors. I love you both and am going to complete the work that I have begun in you both. It is my great love for you, and that which I have chosen both of you to accomplish through my Son that I am calling you both to—*be holy, for I am holy* (I Peter 1:16 NABRE)."*

Tears rolled down my cheeks as I pondered what I had just heard in my heart. A great peace enveloped me as I drifted off to sleep.

In the morning, Tierney and I said our goodbyes to her mother and left for St. Augustine, Florida to a beach house with a room for each of us. God had sent me a number of what I like to call, "heavenly kisses," the most precious being the affirmation from Tierney's mother, Pat. On the drive to St. Augustine, the Lord brought a memory back to my mind. St. Augustine, Florida was the place my parents spent their honeymoon about 50 years earlier. Was this a coincidence? I think not.

We checked into our rooms which had views of the beach and ocean, fireplaces in the corners, and some sweet treats to welcome us. Strolling along the beach at night was one of the fondest memories of our stay there. The night sky was almost alive as a distant storm lit it up with flashes of orange and red. Above us, the stars seemed to have multiplied into a sea of lights that glistened and twinkled. 'A perfect setting,' we thought as we gazed into each other's eyes. Atop the sand dunes, wrapped in God's creation, we embraced and kissed passionately for what seemed like hours. Time stood still as we allowed God's love to flow between us. The purity of our passionate embrace is hard to put into words.

We took a horse and carriage ride through the streets of St. Augustine, Florida, then walked into a small Catholic Church we found that had Eucharistic Adoration. We both knelt, praying and praising God with hearts of gratitude for what He was doing in our lives. After fine dining, we returned to our beach house where we discovered a hammock stretched between two palm trees that became our nest to share our hearts into the wee hours of the morning.

The time of our second date drew to a close and we knew in our hearts that God had ordained a sacred journey for us on the road to a Sacramental Marriage. Never taking God for granted, we were grateful for each day we had with each other.

My May 8, 2011, text message to Tierney read:

"I so long to be fully in your life. I am missing you. I am experiencing such an ache, like I am incomplete. You complete me, my perfect complement. I so enjoy sharing my life with you that it is no longer mine but OURS. I wish I were with you. We would laugh and dance 'til the sun came up in the morning and found us curled up in each other's arms in a hammock under the trees, my dearest Tierney. I LOVE YOU! He is making ALL things NEW.

His plan for us is PERFECT! Full of life. He {God} is the Author of the DANCE our united hearts yearn for . . . YHG (Your Humble Giant)."

My May 11, 2011, text message to Tierney read:

"I am at church by myself, walking the Passion of Christ (stations of the Cross), and when I looked at the fourth image, a Daughter of God the Father comforting His Son on His journey to Calvary, God spoke this to my heart: 'As I sent My daughter to comfort My Only Begotten Son, Jesus, as He carried His cross, so too, David, I have sent my daughter, Tierney, to comfort you and tend to your wounds. Be at peace, my son. I love you.'"

My May 12, 2011, text message to Tierney read:

"My heart beats for you, my beloved. Long have I waited for this moment in time—for the music of the mystical dance of love, for my chosen partner to unlock the chambers of my heart so that they may flow freely with the nectar of love. You are my beloved, my bride-to-be. Drink freely from the springs of my heart—I have both given and entrusted it to you. Bathe in the waters of its beauty. They flow for you and you alone. YHG."

My May 16, 2011, text message to Tierney read:

Prayer from my heart: *"My dearest Heavenly Father, may I please be given the grace to greet each new day's dawning, as the birds do, with melodious songs of joy, thanksgiving, praise, gratitude, and worship to You, Father, and may the voice that unites with mine be the voice of Tierney Hathaway Foster's. I love You, Father. This is my heart's deepest desire. My dearest Heavenly Father, You are making everything new. You are in control. I am so thankful, so grateful, so humbled at what You are doing in my life, and most importantly, whom You have entrusted to my care—Your daughter, Tierney. Oh my Father, such a treasure as this a man could invest his whole life searching for and never find this Treasure of Treasures, and yet You have chosen me to receive this gift of a lifetime. Please Father, grant me the grace to love her as You love her, cherish her as You cherish her, honor her as You honor her ALL the days of my life. Your beloved son, David."*

The Courtship Continues

FOR OUR THIRD date, Tierney wanted to go somewhere where I had special memories with my father, and so we traveled to Maryland's Tilghman Island and the Harrison House for a weekend of fishing. For over 40 years, I fished on the Chesapeake Bay with my father. Tilghman Island was our final fishing trip together, so this was the perfect place.

Memories abounded for me as we arrived in St. Michaels, walking the streets that my mother and father and I had walked so many times in the past. A trip through memory lane in the Nautical Museum, then a delicious seafood meal at the Crab Shack overlooking the river brought our first day to a close.

Bright and early the next morning, we went fishing for big stripers

which it seems were always caught by Tierney. They say, [16]"a picture is worth a thousand words," so the photograph that the captain captured of my 12-inch striper and Tierney's 42-incher really told the whole story. I am not sure how many times I cried tears of joy, but the experience was an amazing time of healing. I have precious memories of fishing with my father, and now I have new ones with my beloved Tierney. God was at it again, making all things new, healing the old, and creating new memories that money cannot buy.

God had also brought Tierney and me back to the Harrison House in Tilghman Island for another purpose—to be the messengers of the answer to the prayers of the matriarch of the Harrison family, Bobbie Harrison. She had prayed for God to send someone to help her family, her husband, and their family business. God had chosen Tierney and me to help them, asking nothing in return. Bobbie Harrison passed away about a year-and-a-half later with grace and an amazing peace through the hope that God had shown her through the "yes" given by Tierney and me. Buddy Harrison, Sr. passed away about two years later, a changed man, a precious and humble son of God the Father. Some of his last words to his son, Buddy, Jr. were, "I know where I am going. I want to go home." He knew God. This God moment in our courtship was only a glimpse of how God was going to use us for His purpose.

We both returned home and another chapter in our book was being penned by the Father. The love poetry kept flowing, and with eager anticipation we planned our next week together, which would be to meet Tierney's sons. One lived in Los Angeles, California, and the other lived in Kona, Hawaii. Both boys wanted to meet me to make sure that I would cherish and protect the heart of their mother. They wanted to check me out to see if I was fit to be the caretaker of such a precious heart as their mother's.

My June 3, 2011, text message to Tierney read:

"Treasured, cherished, and precious are the memories I have stored in the vault of my heart of us. Their value is priceless because money can neither buy nor replace them. Their significance has no earthly measure but rather, a heavenly origin. Books will be written to tell our story, my love. They will impact countless numbers as their message of hope, healing, redemption, and true love, as it was meant to be, pierces the heart of the reader. I love you, my beloved. Thank you, Father, for entrusting to me the heart of your most precious daughter."

My June 14, 2011, text message to Tierney read:

"You are always with me, my love. I carry you in the sanctuary of my heart. Whenever I choose to go there, it is so refreshing, so life-giving. The fragrance soothes my very soul. I go there often throughout my day. I love you, my Dove."

The courtship continued throughout the month of June through a multitude of daily texts and late night interludes, via phone, and always with Tierney reading a Bible verse to me that the Lord put on her heart.

We traveled to Los Angeles, California, where I met Tierney's youngest son. We then traveled to Kona, Hawaii to meet Tierney's other son. Though cautious, they accepted me and trusted me to be the caretaker of their mother's heart. This took time. Throughout this now three-and-a-half-year journey with Tierney's family, many God moments have taken place, allowing me to be there for both her sons and her precious mother who is now almost 96 years old. This again, is a confirmation of God's fingerprints in our courtship, for God's fingerprints are always an exchange of gifts. Tierney was a gift to me and my family. So, too, am I a gift to her and her family.

God was making all things new. He was restoring that which the locust tried to destroy. Each month, we would go to a different place where new memories were created.

Palm Island, Tierney's sanctuary in Florida, was a place of great healing and great pain for her. She had lost her beloved home, her nest in Palm Island, but wanted to take me there to create new memories of hope. We went there in July, 2011, and walked the white sand beaches, holding hands for hours, occasionally stopping along the way to pick up a beautiful seashell or a fossilized shark tooth, and yes, more occasionally to embrace and melt into each other. We treasured these times of solitude and healing as God continued His work in us, preparing us for that special day when we would enter into our Sacramental Marriage.

We longed to be united, but remained surrendered to God's plan and timing.

When we left Palm Island and stepped off the boat, we experienced another "God moment." A precious elderly lady, celebrating her 92nd birthday, came over to us and anointed our heads with oil and the sign of the cross saying, "May God continue to bless your union." Wow! That was both emotionally and spiritually moving.

In August, we flew to Ireland to meet Anne from Direction for Our Times and Father Darragh, the chaplain. The meeting was precious as they got to meet this very special woman that God brought into my life. Treasured was the time we spent with each other, seeing the sights of Ireland—from Dublin to the Cliffs of Moher. Prayer time with both

Anne and Father Darragh was beyond words. It was holy; it was ordained. The readings of each Mass seemed to be selected by God Himself. He spoke His confirmation to each of our hearts about what He was doing in our lives, both individually and as a couple. Anne's words, "Be patient and wait on the Lord, David," still echoes in my heart. "She is His gift to you."

As we continued our courtship, I asked Tierney and her oldest son as well as her son's future wife, to join me in Quarryville, Pennsylvania to attend a [17] *Theology of the Body* week-long course taught by my very dear friend, Christopher West. Christopher had been on an almost ten-year journey with me and saw how God had healed and restored me as well as how He had brought into my life, at the right moment, my precious Tierney. The [18] *Theology of the Body* teachings, as Christopher West presents them, were a major help in my healing, sexually. They helped me to truly understand what God had meant for marriage from the beginning. This week-long course, as part of our courtship, impacted all of us as the eyes of our hearts were opened to the true mystical beauty of the biblical dance of love which is what marriage is meant to be.

Meeting My Children

ONE OF THE most difficult parts of the courtship between Tierney and me was being obedient to my spiritual director's instruction to protect this relationship, to not share about it with any family members or friends until the proper time. I knew this was wise counsel, meant to protect the children, and without the help of God it would be impossible to live out for one-and-one-half years, but live it out we did. I knew in my heart that I could not share the news of our courtship until after my daughter Mai-Lynn's wedding in September, 2012.

So we waited until two days after Mai-Lynn's wedding to share with all of my children about our courtship. Joy, tears, hugs, laughter, and comments like, "I knew something was different about you, dad," and "So that's why you would always be talking to someone late into the night" all poured forth. They were all happy for their dad, and yet deep in their hearts, they were sad for the ending of the spark of hope of possible reconciliation between myself and their mother. They did not make the choices that brought us to this moment, we did. Allowing the children to express their range of emotions throughout our courtship until our marriage was essential for their healing and acceptance.

Through God's grace working in both Tierney and me, the children not only ended up accepting, but embracing our union and trusting God for the healing of our family.

Our courtship in front of the children when they were looking, and especially when we thought they were not looking, always had to remain pure and respectful of both God's teachings as well as respectful toward their mother. At the end of this book, you will have the opportunity to read lessons learned and about parenting in a blended family. I believe this portion of the book has great wisdom that God taught us during our journey and we want to share it with you. Our children are precious treasures that God Himself has entrusted us to be caretakers of. Please read these sections and take them to heart so that you may live them out.

It was now January of 2013, with almost two years of courtship, and the final decrees of annulment were still winding their way through the Church's process. I asked God a question after Mass one day, "May I order the engagement ring?" to which the still, quiet voice in my heart spoke, "Yes, you may, David, but you must put it in your safe and not show it to Tierney until it is time." I felt lighter than air and giddy as a school boy. My Heavenly Father had said, "Yes." So without delay, I went to the jewelry store the next day and chose both the stone and the setting. Feeling "excited," was putting it mildly. I was bubbling over. It took about two months or so to custom-make the engagement ring, and when I picked it up, I knew in an instant where I would ask for my beloved Tierney's hand in marriage. I would again take her to the small church in Linwood, New Jersey where we prayed together for two hours on our first date. In front of the Blessed Sacrament in Adoration, I would ask for the hand of my beloved Tierney.

The Lord's timing took until May, but it was perfect. A friend of Tierney's needed prayer, so I suggested that we go to the same Catholic Church in Linwood, New Jersey where we also prayed for friends before, and she agreed.

After we knelt for about an hour or so in prayer, we got up to leave, and there in front of our Lord in the monstrance, I knelt and asked for my beloved Tierney's hand in marriage. She replied, "I have to think about it." Knowing the quips of my beloved, I was not phased one bit and exposed the ring I had made for her. She lit up and said, "Yes, I will marry you." We both shed tears of joy as we embraced in front of our Lord. God had led us on a two-and-one-half-year journey of courtship, obedience, and surrender that now was going to culminate into His love story of His children, David and Tierney.

The Wedding Day

EVERYTHING HAD TO be perfect. I immediately called my spiritual director, Monsignor John Esseff, to ask him to preside over our wedding, to which he responded, "David, do not wait for me. Get married as soon as possible." So we set the wedding date for July 26, 2013. Monsignor King and Father Dave would preside, and only family and very close friends would be invited. Being Catholic, I needed to get married in our Catholic Church; however, the heart's dream of my wife-to-be, who is an evangelical Christian, was to be married in our gazebo on the pond. She forsook her heart's desire and agreed to the wedding at the Catholic church across the street. But you see, I always want to fulfill the desires of her heart, so unbeknownst to her, I had the gazebo decked out in flowers with about 100 of our friends waiting. A pastor friend of ours met us there, a witness to the renewal of our vows, so it was not *either/or*, but *both/and* for the wedding venue.

My July 26, 2013, text message to Tierney (on the day of our wedding) read:

"Good morning, my beloved! Today is the day the Lord has made and ordained to be a day of celebration, of rejoicing, of thanksgiving, of dancing.

> *The bridegroom is calling, come my beloved, this is our day to give testimony to the love story scripted from our hearts, penned there by the Father, unveiled by the Mother, and lived out through the Son. I am yours, my Dove. May our Lord Jesus Christ love you purely through me all the days of your life and eternally with Him. YHG."*

The day arrived and was absolutely picturesque, the perfect day for our wedding. A white horse-drawn carriage arrived at the farmhouse to bring her one mile to the church. She was radiant, aglow in the Lord as she and her best friend, Andra, rode in the carriage, making their way to the church. My very good friend, Mark Forrest, an Irish tenor, sang the songs we had chosen, including *Ave Maria*, the song that my grandfather used to sing in church. My lips quivered and the tears rolled down my face as I thought of him, my mother, and my father—all of whom had gone home to be with the Lord. I believe they were present in spirit, along with a cloud of witnesses.

Monsignor King gave his homily on marriage. It was prophetic in nature as the Holy Spirit spoke through him of the truths of what God the Father had ordained. Tierney and I clasped hands as the tears rolled. Then it was time for our written wedding vows. Here is what we spoke to each other:

Bride's Commitment:

Bride's Commitment

"MHG" "My Humble Giant"

I thank you for coming into my life and bringing hope, healing, and joy. God has so gifted me beyond my expectation and entrusted me with a most beautiful heart in you. I pledge to always protect it and to ride tandem with you in the life and work God has called us to.

I give you my heart, my energies, my gifts, my future, and my safekeeping. I will love you with a pure heart and serve our Lord side by side.

I respect and honor you as my head, the head of the family, and the spiritual leader He has placed over me to guide and protect me.

Thank you for your "yes" almost two and one half years ago. Today, I again pledge you my "yes" everyday that God unites us on this earth.

I Love You,

Jimmey
"your Dove"

Groom's Commitment/Prayer:

Heavenly Father,

With all my heart, I want to thank You for entrusting to me the heart of Your beloved daughter.

Help me, Father, to realize each day just how precious she is to You, and then, with your grace, allow me Father to love her purely, honor her in all I do, treasure her as the priceless jewel of Your heart, woo her as Your beloved, and protect her with all the Armor of Christ.

Allow me, Father, to lead her with the heart of Christ, love her with the heart of Mary, protect her with the heart of Joseph, counsel her with the heart of the Holy Spirit, hear her with the ears of wisdom, defend her with the courage and strength of St. Michael the Archangel, treasure her with Your heart, the heart of the Father, and lay down my life for her, my sister, my bride, as Jesus did.

Tierney, these things I pray. I also pledge to live out in love all the days of my life.

David YHG

We said our "I do's." We were husband and wife, bonded in the covenant of a Sacramental Marriage. A new chapter in our lives began. The white horse-drawn carriage took us from the church, down the winding lane toward the pond where our friends waited. As the carriage came to a stop just around the corner from the gazebo, my new wife asked, "Who are all these people and why did we stop?" Then, as her mind was putting the pieces together, the music she had always wanted to be played at her wedding started and she said, "not either / or," and I replied, "both / and" as we walked arm in arm to meet all of our family and friends as husband and wife. We made our way out onto the gazebo over the water which looked like a floating flower garden. There, Pastor Al met and congratulated us, and proceeded to preside over our wedding vow renewals. When he announced us as "husband and wife," the Christian rock song, "Stomp," started to play. We donned our dark sunglasses (hidden there by me earlier) and danced over the bridge to our waiting family and friends.

Love at First Flight—a Plane Fairy Tale, is our story of seeing God at work in our lives. His mercy, His forgiveness, and His love are so great for each and every one of us. We hope that our story of hope, restoration, and resurrection is planted deep in the soil of your heart so that God may grow it. ALL things are possible with God. Seek Him with *all* of your heart and then watch Him work.

May God bless each and every one of you who read our story and may He grant you the eyes and ears of the heart to see and hear Him at work in your life.

With all of our love,

David and Tierney Abel

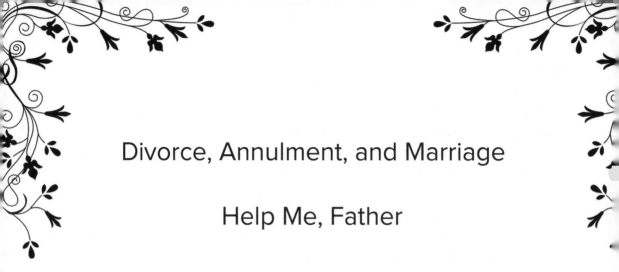

Divorce, Annulment, and Marriage

Help Me, Father

BEING RAISED AS a Roman Catholic, I knew I could never divorce. There was the shame, the guilt, the failure, the children, and more importantly, I knew and was taught that *God hated divorce*. The words at the marriage ceremony clearly rang in my ears, "What God has joined, let no man separate." But here I was, living in two rooms under my mother-in-law's house, the house my former spouse and I built for her to use after being told to move out for the third time. My former spouse of 30 years wanted a divorce and filed for one. She had made her decision and proceeded on the path she had chosen. Then one day, walking from the bedroom, I heard the still, quiet voice in my heart speak these words to me, "David, if you walk this walk, it will become your story and I will use it to help a multitude." I knew in an instant that the walk He meant was walking out of a civil divorce. Initially, I cried out, "No Father, not me, not this." Then, the tears rolled down my cheeks and I lowered my head in full surrender to the will of my Father in heaven. "Not my will be done, but Your will be done, Father, for You know what is best for me, the children, and my former spouse. I surrender to Your will, Father."

"Jesus, I trust in You," was the cry of my heart. A comforting, soothing peace came over me as I placed it all in the Lord's hands and let go.

The divorce proceedings dragged on and on with lawyer's letters, arbitration, etc. It was one of the most painful journeys of my life. It lasted over two-and-a-half years. It was also one of the most grace-filled, healing periods of my life because full surrender to God's will in my life opened up the doors of my heart for the great work the Father wanted to do in me. He was healing me as a man, a son, a father, and a husband-to-be, taking me back to the way He created me to be from the beginning, chaste and pure. He actually restored my virginity as I became a *new creation in Christ*. He defeated lust within me, purified, and changed my disordered desires into a pure desire for Him who is the source of all love. Prioritizing that relationship was first in my journey of healing. God greatly desired to be my first love. I chose to put Him first, and in doing so, began to realize that through that ever-deepening relationship with God, not only personally, but intimately, all other relationships in my life received His love through me—to the children, to my friends, and yes, even to my former spouse. God taught me that the deeper the intimacy in my relationship with Him, the richer the streams of unconditional love that flowed from my heart to everyone He brought into my life. He taught me to always *respond* with love, sometimes even tough love, but never to *react*. For when I react, I take the enemy's bait. He also taught me to see my former spouse the way He sees her—an eight-year-old precious little girl before the world wounded her. This really helped me to separate her reactions from the precious daughter of God which is truly who she is.

Do not go into the world, into the arms of another, to find healing and hope. Run to God. He is the answer. He is the One who can truly heal, restore, renew, resurrect, and yes, make *all* things new again if we but run into His arms, surrendering all to Him. God is the answer. He is the source of true love, not another. When we go to the world to fill the great ache of our heart, or to another to fill that which *only* God can fill, it is like drinking saltwater, thinking it will quench our thirst. In reality, it will kill us. Too many times, people seek the answer in another person and end up repeating the same mistakes that brought down the first marriage to divorce. God was not the central source of love in the relationship. It takes three in a marriage. God must be at the core (heart) of the relationship or it is doomed to fail as the weight of filling that great ache of the heart is put on the other and crushes that person. I again repeat that only God and an intimate relationship with Him can fill the void.

My two-and-a half-year journey through divorce, with God, was one of amazing healing, renewal, rebirth, restoration, and resurrection. God used this time to teach me, first and foremost, how to receive His love, fully embracing my identity in Him as His beloved son. This is why God must be first in each and every person's life, not fitting God into our busy schedule, but building our schedule around our time with God. This is right-ordered.

What the world offers through all of its addictions is counterfeit to the truth that God and God alone *is* sufficient. It is through that obedience in love to His first commandment to *love the Lord your God with all your heart, with all your soul, with all your mind, and with all your strength* (Mark 12:30 NABRE) that *all* other relationships are ordered. We then become pure vessels of His love which flows into every other relationship—our spouse, our children, and the world.

God's Word tells us that only if a marriage is unlawful are two (that look joined in this bond) able to separate and be open to God's will in their lives. Each can then live as chaste, single persons, fully and completely surrendered to the fact that this may be God's plan for their lives or that God may bring together, in the Sacrament of Marriage, "helpmeets"—husband and wife. Because the Roman Catholic Church teaches and adheres to the truth of God's Word, the Church knows that it cannot divide what God has joined together. Therefore, Church leaders go back to the beginning of the first marriage and seek to understand, through the guidance of the Holy Spirit, if it was truly a "Sacramental Marriage," an unbreakable covenant between each of the persons and God. A sacrament is an outward sign, established by Christ, to receive grace. God instituted the Sacrament of Marriage, starting with the first Adam and Eve. The process, through which the Catholic Church discerns whether or not a marriage, in the world's eyes, was truly sacramental, is called, "the annulment process."

I knew nothing about the Catholic Church's annulment process, but the Lord, through His mercy, wanted to take me on a journey of learning about this beautiful truth and the healing process it is meant to be. The Church takes both parties back to the time when they said their "I do's" at the original ceremony to discern if they were both fully capable of entering into the sacred Sacramental Covenant of Marriage. The Church realizes that anyone can say, "I do." Most unions between a man and a woman can produce the fruit of children, but this does not make it a Sacramental Marriage. This process helps both parties go back to the beginning to understand if they were in a state of grace and in full knowledge of the covenant with God as they were entering into when they first said, "I do."

This process helped me greatly understand the state of my soul at the age of 21 when I said, "I do." I was deep in sexual addition, pornography, and acting out in fantasy, which then led to reality during the marriage. I truly had no idea what marriage was and what it was to be—a sign post and invitation to the eternal exchange of pure, unconditional love which is heaven. God took me on a "Great Adventure," as I like to call it, to teach me the truth about marriage and the sexual embrace of a husband and wife which must always reflect God's love—free, total, faithful, and most importantly, fruitful (open to God's gift of life, a child). God took my disordered desire for pornography and reordered it to a burning desire for truth about why God made us male and female and why the union of the two in the Sacrament of Marriage is a one-flesh union. This truth is found in God's Holy Word, the Bible, and is so beautifully broken open in the [19] *Theology of the Body*, presented by Christopher West, Jason Evert, and so many more who have found this beautiful truth that God has revealed to His children in His Word.

Witnesses from the time of my first marriage were asked to share their insight related to my ability to enter into the Sacred Covenant. All this information was gathered over a nine-month period. Then the Church, through its appointed advocate and defender of the bond, surrendered to the guidance of the Holy Spirit and it was deemed, after an additional three-month period, that both parties in the first marriage (although the union produced good in children and was a relationship between a man and a woman), were not in a state of grace with full knowledge of what a true Sacramental Marriage was to be. Therefore, the marriages of both were annulled, by the grace and mercy of God, through His Church. I was fully surrendered to the decision of the Church and the guidance of the Holy Spirit. If the Church's decision was that they could not consider annulment in both cases, then I would pray for the grace to walk the rest of my life as a chaste, single person. However, if the Church ruled an annulment in both, then I would continue to open up and allow God to prepare me and teach me what a Sacramental Marriage truly looked like. And prepare me and teach me, He did!

What is a Sacramental Marriage?

GOD INSTITUTED THE Sacrament of Marriage, in its purest form, to be a foretaste of the One Marriage in Heaven between the Bridegroom, Christ, and each and every member of His one Body, the Church. God created us male and female in His image and likeness so that through this one-flesh union in the Sacrament of Marriage, the eternal exchange of love between the Father and Son which is the outpouring of the third Person in the Holy Trinity, the Holy Spirit, may be foreshadowed. A right-ordered, true reflection of God's unconditional love in a marriage takes place when the husband is in full and constant communion (common union) with the heart of God, daily being an open vessel through which God the Father loves His daughter, God the Son loves His sister, and God the Holy Spirit purely loves His bride. Likewise, the wife is in full and constant communion with the heart of God, daily being that open vessel through which God the Father loves His Son, God the Son loves His brother, and God the Holy Spirit purely loves His bride. If there is a problem in the marriage, the roots of that problem are always found in a breakdown in the relationship of one or both with God. They are out of communion with the heart of God. God is the total source of all unity in all marriages and when there is disunity and division, the enemy is in the marriage, working to divide and conquer.

This understanding of Sacramental Marriage has allowed God to prepare me for the person He had chosen for me. I never went "out into the world" and looked for someone to date. That was something I could never do. It would have destroyed me. I could not allow more wounding to my heart. So, through this two-and-a-half years of isolation, God drew me into the one relationship that satisfied—that ever-deepening, intimate relationship with Him. He prepared me for my bride, His daughter, His sister, His beloved Tierney, which is the story you just read, *Love at First Flight—A Plane Fairy Tale*.

The Children of Blended Families

Seventeen children, seven grandchildren, and growing. Our combined family of 12 daughters (ranging in age from 12 to 40) and five sons (ranging in age from 12 to 35) certainly comprise a *full quiver* (Psalm 127:5 KJV). Parenting them the way God desires us to with His heart requires total surrender to God, allowing Him to parent through us because each of the children are first and foremost His children which He entrusts to our care. God has taught me so much through this journey.

Following is a synopsis of the wisdom that God revealed to me—lessons learned and lived.

1. Recognizing that a former spouse is God's precious son or daughter (no matter the words or actions that come from them), is the key to loving them as God loves them. They may *react* in many ways that are not of God because of wounds they have. We must always *respond* in love, even tough love, setting safe boundaries and asking the Holy Spirit to speak truth in love through us. The children want to know that you still love their father or mother and never want to be exposed to the toxins of anger and unforgiveness. We, as

human beings, cannot do this on our own. We must turn to God always and ask Him to help us. The extent to which we love our former spouse purely, is the extent to which we love God. We are not called to love their actions or words, but we are called to love them and pray for them as often as God brings them to our minds. Take *all* your wounds and feelings to God and share them with Him, allowing Him to heal them. Do not take them into the world through others.

2. Children are *always* watching and listening. More than our words, they *hear* our actions loudly. It is imperative that the children are protected and safe in the home. Their well-being must be the first priority to all who parent them. They must always see our love and respect for their mother or father, our former spouse.

3. Never guilt, control, or manipulate the children. Always allow them to express their love freely to both parents and spouses of their parents. Encourage and support the children in their relationship with the former spouse. This is imperative for their healthy development.

4. Let children be children, playing, interacting, and encouraging them as father and mother. Never put them in the middle or involve them in adult matters between spouses.

5. Do not try to satisfy your curiosity about what the former spouse is doing by asking the children questions. It damages children and can hurt the parent, too. Unless a child is in danger with the former spouse, stop them when they try to tell you things. Change the talk to something about their life and

yours. Setting this tone of a safe boundary is imperative to raising healthy children—teaching them what is and what is not appropriate.

6. Never coerce the children into taking sides. There are no sides in a broken family. There are just broken people—mother, father, and children—who each need to experience God's unconditional love in all situations.

7. Allow the children time to heal, and love them where they are in their life's journey. We are not called to "fix it," because we are not God. We are called to love unconditionally as God loves each of us.

8. Know and be assured that truth and love always prevail, so always lead a life that reflects this because it reflects Christ who is fully both.

9. Our *Number One* vocation as a separated or single parent is our children. They must come first, above all else, because their healing, safety, and future are directly connected to how we both love and invest in them. If God chooses to bring a helpmeet into our lives as He did for Adam, we are to be open to the gift but always surrendered to His will for us. We are not to be constantly running and looking for someone. This is not only unhealthy for us, but most importantly, it is unhealthy for children who see people coming and going in and out of your life. This wounds the family even more. Children want and need both parents equally. That is the way God created the family unit. In a broken family unit, it is imperative that equal time be given to both in a spirit of cooperation, always looking for what is best for the children. Always seek God's counsel, especially if one of the parents is unhealthy or not safe. Seek the counsel of godly people on this journey, always turning to God's Word which is Truth and Love.

10. Be truthful. If and when your children ask questions, always ask God to help you share only what is helpful and never what is hurtful to the other. Only share what God reveals to you as healthy, healing truth. "The devil is in the details," as the saying goes, and when we share too much, we confuse the children, and more often than not, we hurt the other parent *and* ourselves.

11. In conclusion, parenting is a sacred trust where God Himself entrusts His children to our care to raise, guide, protect, and love with His heart. It was not a mistake that God chose us to be parents. It is a mistake not to seek and enlist God's help in this great commission where God is the source of all we need and we are the vessels of His love, mercy, compassion, forgiveness, counsel, and wisdom. *With God all things are possible* (Matthew 19:26 KJV), even in a broken, earthly family, as we come to realize that we are all members of the family of God.

Lessons Learned

1. Never *react*. Always *respond* in love. Go to God for help because He is love.

2. You cannot separate truth and love because they are both fully Christ.

3. [20]"Let go and let God." Understanding that "I am not God," and letting go, allowing God to be God, set me free from trying to "fix it."

4. It takes two—a man and a woman—to fully and completely give their total "yes" to make a marriage. Yes, first and foremost, to their first love, God and that relationship, and then to each other.

5. Yes, a non-sacramental marriage can become a sacramental marriage through the total surrender of both parties, individually, to their relationship with God as their primary source of love. He then can resurrect, renew, and restore all things.

6. Divorce is never the answer. God is the answer. Divorce is not truth. God is truth. Understanding what an annulment is greatly helped me heal from the stigma of the world's term, "divorce." Understanding the truth about a Sacramental Marriage where God is the source to both parties, individually

first, then to each other, prepared me for the great gift of the heart of God's daughter, my wife, Tierney.

7. You cannot fix the other person. However, you must always be open to God's bountiful mercy in healing you. There is no earthly marriage in heaven, but only one marriage—that of Christ to His Bride, His Church—all those who are members of His One Body. God's *Number One* objective is to bring us all home to Him. That is why He sent His only Son to die for us, paying the price for our choice to sin; thus, He was the ransom for all.

8. [21]"The family that prays together stays together" is a slogan we have heard before. It is also a truth we all must live out all the days of our lives as God provides strength and is our source, our all in all. With *God all things are possible* (Matthew 19:26 NABRE). Without Him, nothing is possible.

9. The courtship should *never* end once you are married if God is at the core (heart) of the relationship. He is always wooing, treasuring, and cherishing the heart of His beloved through the other—"That's you."

10. Another person, another relationship is never the answer. Only God is the answer that lasts and fulfills.

11. Dating is dangerous. Courtship should be the intent of the heart because it is the dance of pure love that leads to marriage if it is of God.

12. The <u>past</u> is in God's mercy. To go there only causes despair because God does not live in the past. The past is a trap the enemy uses to punish us. When we go to God and ask for forgiveness with a contrite heart, He not only forgives us, but restores us anew. Anyone who holds us to our past or uses our past

against us is not in right relationship with God, but is being used by the enemy of our soul. The key to freedom is forgiving ourselves because, in not forgiving ourselves, there is a grave sin that separates us from the healing balm of God's love. As my spiritual director told me, "The past is dead, David. Leave it buried. Every time you dig it up, it stinks."

The <u>future</u> is in God's providence. To go there causes you to "play God." God does not live in the future. I call it the "what if" roller coaster ride you cannot seem to get off. "What if he this, or she that? What if they this or they that?" This roller coaster ride is caused by a lack of faith in God and His providence. Fear is faith in the wrong kingdom.

The <u>present</u> is God's gift to be lived in love. Open the gift at every moment and live it with God as His great adventure in love. Know that the enemy of our soul is always trying to rob and steal this most precious of gifts from us. Wake up and live the abundant life.

13. Connection with the One Body of Christ during your journey here on earth is critically important, such as small faith-sharing groups that meet once a week (or more often) to break open the *Bread of Life* (the Word of God). Daily Scripture reading and meditation on God's Word, as well as reading books that God directs you to that help you heal and grow, are also very important. Unplugging from unhealthy people, television, the Internet, etc. and plugging into godly things will change you and set you free. I call it a "detoxing."

14. Looking at pornography in any form is adultery. It is wrongfully using God's daughter, and the daughter of the mother and father He chose, for perverted

desires. It is sexual abuse of the person who is created in the image and likeness of God, and so it is also an abuse of Almighty God Himself when His creation is abused.

15. Never compromise yourself by putting yourself in a situation or position that could lead you to fall during the courtship period. Purity and chastity are the open channels of God's love to the other. If we fall, we block those channels, so immediately seek God's mercy by asking His forgiveness, forgiving yourself, and asking God for the grace not to fall again. Then stay away from situations or places where you could be tempted to fall. God's grace is sufficient, but it also requires our active participation and "yes" to God's will for us to remain pure and chaste. Do not take the bait of the enemy of our soul that lies and says, "I have fallen. I might as well continue to fall. I have failed." Go to God in repentance. Receive His mercy and grace to start anew.

16. Transparency in a marriage is absolutely essential. Nothing should be hidden (e.g., emails, texts, website visits, telephone calls, and messages). For when there are secrets, the enemy of our soul gains power and the seeds of division take root. This does not include sharing the past which is in God's mercy. Today can be a new start to the life God greatly desires for us to have—the abundant life in Him, with Him, and through Him.

17. The love that finds its source in, through, and with God, is always free, not controlling, nor manipulative. "Total" is the full gift of oneself to the other spouse. Being "faithful," first in a primary relationship with God, and then to your spouse, is critically important. Being "fruitful" produces the life-giving fruit of love that is tasted by all who meet the couple, inspiring in others that

which the couple has—a personal and intimate relationship with God and each other. God's love casts out all fear in a relationship.

18. Do not assume to know the mind of God and justify sin by moving in together during the courtship period or getting engaged before an annulment decision is handed down. Yes, the perfect way is always waiting on God to open and close the chapters (windows) of our lives. Do not get ahead of God. Follow His lead, His steps. His promptings are always in perfect harmony with His Word, the sacred Scriptures.

Conclusion

ALL THINGS ARE possible through God who is love. Trust in Him, walk with him, and allow Him to be your total source, and He will grant you the deepest desires of your heart as you become one with Him.

PART III

The "Text Book"

The "Text Book" is a window through which we peer into the masterpiece of the heart. It is candid expression which "courts" the heart of the lover in true and vulnerable transparency. It chooses to risk loss and love in order to experience love as it was meant to be. We have delicately lifted the veil of our "texting love language" to inspire those who love; to express, embrace, and nurture the poetry of the heart.

First Months of Texts—
The Expression of Love

FIRST TEXT—February 26, 2011:

> Me: Hi..just 4 the fun of it..a text! It was very encouraging 2 meet a man of mission + character as yrslf. C..it is ok 2 abbrev while textg.God Bless..Tierney
>
> Sent: Feb 26
>
> David Z Abel: I am doing this just for you, and it is an honor. Dito thank you. You were a healing balm to my heart. God bless, david

Be kind . . . I feel like I am back in school learning how to type. This is my fourth text ever. Thank you for inspiring me. I will always respond to you. David

Working on some of those 1,000 questions. How was your day? I truly am looking forward to the next time we talk. I am so sorry it may not be until Mon. night. Please do not hesitate 2 text. I will try to respond. U are my special text pal. David

Tierney challenged me to make Text #100 memorable, so here is what I sent: *Fourscore and 99 texts ago I had the honor and privilege of meeting a very beautiful woman who allowed me to open a very special place in my heart. She entered slowly and tenderly, bringing with her a healing peace, joy, and laughter I have not experienced in a long time. She is my very special friend whom I am learning to treasure in a very special way. Thank you for sharing the gift of this part of your life with me. Thank you also for allowing me inside your heart as your very special friend. David*

Tierney asked me the question, *"How was hunting?"* I responded, *"I had a great time, however, I was thinking of you and was distracted so I missed half of the birds."* She replied, *"Oh no, David. I cannot be a distraction in your life. You must stay focused on what God has called you to. I want to be the wind in your sails that affirms what God is doing in your life. I cannot be a distraction. I want to stand beside you and be your greatest cheering section, encouraging you onto what God has anointed you to do."*

I want to help you, David, defend your purity and protect your walk of chastity. Tierney

R u slowing down 2 day 2 allow God to show u just how much He loves U? I am taking a walk in the woods, been a long time. David

This morn. at Mass I was filled with such Peace it was intoxicating. I'm still floating. I am sitting at the back of my property looking over God's beauty and texting my very special friend. Wywh. Thank you My very special friend . . . David

"It was my Mother who wanted this for you, David. She loves you and she wants you to dance slowly, savoring it, one step at a time. We will be with you." David (from Jesus to my heart).

The sun is setting, rays of light are cascading across the endless ocean, and pockets of colors erupt in the crashing waves like a symphony of precious gems being cast upon the shore. For a moment, you cannot breathe, time stands still, and then it happens . . . you experience a Divine moment with your Divine Lover. David

The petals of the heart of a beautiful woman . . . she is a mysterious flower who has allowed me the great honor of a glimpse of her inner radiant beauty. Thanks. YSF {Your Special Friend} David

God is loving your Mother through you. You are precious in His sight, Tierney. His love for you is beyond measure—you bring such a joy to His heart. It is an honor and a pleasure to get to know you. YSF, David

The Lord sang to my heart all day—through the CD you gave me. It spoke about my life's journey, your life's journey, and in a special way, our life's journey at this time. Wow! Yes, the tears flowed freely—they cleansed my soul as I experienced His love. David

There is no such thing as a coincidence; it is just a failure to see God at work in our lives. The flowers were delivered to you on the date from the Father to His daughter just to let her know how much He loves you. I was merely the instrument. David

I want to be the wind in your sails to help you accomplish all God has called you to. Tierney

Thank you for saying u want 2 b the wind in my sail to help me accomplish all God has called me 2. I want 2 b the wind that allows u 2 soar . . . good night. David

I stood out on my balcony, breathing in God's beauty, listening to His voice in the sounds of nature. They trumpeted in harmony—a new springtime is coming. YSF, David

The batteries of my heart are fully charged to overflowing. I have a confidence in my step, clarity in my vision, and determination to complete what God has put in my heart. Thanks so very much for your very special and treasured wind in my sails. Your feathers are growing back. I would be honored to be the wind beneath your wings that takes you to the highest heights. God has great plans for you. He has been preparing you for His purpose . . . YVSF {Your Very Special Friend}. Thanks for sharing your heart with me. David

You made my heart come alive with Hope! The song that kept saying, "Trust Me" is what the Lord keeps speaking in my heart every time I asked the question, "Why, Lord?" over six years of this painful desert journey. I know you can relate. Then along came a very special GIFT, my special friend. Thank you, Father. David

Good morning! Quality time with the special someone in my life is second only to my quality time with God; for it is from that relationship that the fire of His love flows . . . YSF. Thanks for being you! David

Walking the pups, my time 4 prayer and reflection . . . wish you were here so I could see your face, your smile, hear your voice asking questions . . . be FREE—be you!!! It is intoxicating . . . scent of a truly BEAUTIFUL WOMAN. YSF, David

I am to tell you that you are putting the music back in my heart, from mourning to joy . . . a spirit of heaviness to a spirit of praise. Thank you, my special friend. Tierney

I hear the voice of the Holy Spirit within you and it brings me great comfort. David

U made me smile, I think I blushed. I know my heart skipped a beat . . . you r awesome!!! Good morn . . . mvsffff. David

With all my heart, I want to see your face, gaze endlessly into your eyes, and just snuggle into the captivating beauty of your HEART! David

"His mercies are new every morning." I am loving your heart which I am getting to know. I am respecting your integrity and I am sharing our passion. Tierney

Unveiling the mystery of your beauty is a great honor . . . my heart skipped a beat just thinking about it. David

Six billion people in the world. How is it I met the one that is captivating my heart on an airplane ride to Atlanta? Thank you, Father! David

Earth-moving, my dear! Tierney

I have a new name for you . . . "my humble giant." It's just for me to use. MHG! Tierney

You give significance to my life already! Tierney

You heap accolades on me that I don't deserve, but thank you . . . learning to receive—chore for the rest of my life. Tierney

Thanks for your heart. Woo mine softly and slowly. I have been in labor and travail. With birth, there is still discomfort. Do not be afraid, though. Tierney

I have been set away in that place where eagles have to break their ingrown beaks and pluck their feathers. Tierney

One month and 327 texts ago, life as I had known it changed—a new springtime had begun. Life was emerging deep within me. Colors were more vibrant; laughter reverberated throughout my very soul. To what or to whom do I attribute this time of amazing GRACE in my life? It is to my heavenly Father that I offer all the thanksgiving for it was He who entrusted His most precious gift to me one month ago . . . YOU! YVSF, David

You are extraordinary. What we are experiencing is Divine. Thank you for lavishing the Father's love on me. I covet the same for you my "Imported" Humble Giant. Tierney

I am lying here in awe of what God is doing. It is a mystical dance of LOVE . . . two hearts united in One—His! Your text is so true. I am filled with such peace. YVSF, David

Funny that I am just lying here thinking the same and making sure that I am where I need to be with Him in all the secret unknown places of my heart. Tierney

Wow! You are sending me Divine heavenly kisses this morning. You are wooing my heart in a very tender, special way. Thank you, Father, for allowing me to trust Tierney with the key to that very special place in my heart. I feel so protected in her tender hands. She, Father, is a GIFT beyond my dreams. Thank you so much again, Father! David

The morning light has brought clarity to what I tried to share last night. It is the Divine Lover within me who is courting and wooing your heart. The passion of His heart is my heart—they beat as one. David

Sounds great. Just finishing putting kids 2 bed . . . "Mr. Mom" had a looooong day, lot of fun but whew I need a drink of your life-giving water to refresh. David

Scent is for candles for your room . . . allow me to lead in purity. This is for your experience of God's love for you. He wants you to be at peace, resting in His love for you. I am merely setting the atmosphere for Him to shower down His grace on you. David

How grows your feathers? Can you feel the new life's growth emerging? I can see it from afar and it is dazzlingly radiant! Have a great day. Spread your wings and allow the "Breath of God" to dry them and gently caress them. YSF, David

Wondering if Prince Charming can come to the rescue soon? Tierney

Oh, my goodness! You are killing me! I just do not know what to say. I am so overwhelmed and loved. Thank you! XOXOXO. Tierney

Your good morning text melted my heart. I am so honored. Thank you! I will treasure your heart and protect it with all that I am. For this purpose, I have been called . . . I accept, Lord. It is my honor and privilege. YVSF, David

This day has been so powerful, so Spirit filled, much being accomplished . . . so many confirmations . . . heading 2 meeting totally focused, empowered and sharp . . . no distractions just a beautiful wind in my sails . . . thank u. David

Floating on ether—love is in the air. It's a new SPRINGTIME! Wish you were here. Ahhh— tomorrow. David

David, you are Beloved by the Father and by me. Thank you for being OPEN to find me. Tierney.

You have made your home within my heart, my Dove. It is the dwelling place of the Lord— the special place in my heart He has chosen for you. No one else may occupy it—it was created just for you! You are the perfect fit! Your Beloved. David

I never knew the breadth, the width, and the depth of heaven until I tasted it with you! Good morning, my Beloved. David

It is so right to give you security so that you feel safe. It is so very close so that nothing can ever come between us. It is life-giving as all that I have freely flows into you and you into me. It is holy, as God Himself wraps us together in His heavenly cocoon of love and protection. Did you feel it? I did. Your Beloved. David

Good morning, my Dove! Awake overwhelmed at the significance of what we just experienced, confident in what was spoken. Cherish each memory and taste them throughout your day as precious drips of dew from the fruit of our mountaintop experience with God. I love you. David

We are joined together in a Bond of Gratitude to God . . . yes, for all the yes's—this is your 7th year. His perfect number—a year of fulfillment, of promises, and quiet, secret dreams. I love you. Tierney

Response to Tierney's question, *"What is deep water?" Waters that are unknown, uncharted, deep within our very souls . . . new depths that we have not yet gone to, yet devoid of fear as God Himself is taking us there. The beauty is beyond words. What I believe we are both experiencing in nervous moments. Then God sends us a confirmation, a heavenly kiss, and so we hold His hand a little tighter and whisper in His ear, "I trust you, Daddy." In His still, quiet voice, He responds, "Be not afraid, my child. I am your God, your Father. I am in control. Be not afraid—Trust Me." You are so special to me, Tierney. May God shower down His graces on you today. YVSF, David*

This weekend, I got to experience God's handiwork first-hand and it was exhilarating. It took my breath away. I was in wonder and awe at your beauty—seeing it first from a distance, then up close, then in the rapture of your embrace. I was in the Garden with the woman who was created by the Hand of God just for me! Thank you, Father. David

Miss u xoxoxo . . . your beauty has captivated my heart . . . I am yours my beloved. David

A portion of the poem in my heart for u . . . your eyes are hazel green pools of shimmering water that beckons me to enter and dive deep . . . I want to explore their depths and drink from their purity for the rest of my life . . . they are refreshing life-giving waters as He has made them sacred my sister, my Love. David

Just left spiritual direction with Monsignor. ALLLLLL . . . GREAT! Driving for 2.5 hrs—can fill you in if u call. He prayed so beautifully 4 us and our relationship . . . his words . . . GOD's Hand chose her for you and you for her . . . YOU ARE SOULMATES . . . I LOVE YOU. David

Good morning, my Dove! The cool, refreshing waters of the wellspring of my HEART await you. Whenever you need to refresh, renew, and quench your thirst, come to the life-giving waters of my heart. It is your private oasis. Bathe in its waters—they are yours. Your Beloved. David

Heaven and earth touched on a plane ride to Atlanta. The Divine Author turned the page of a new chapter in my life. He enfleshed the desires of my heart. It is you, Tierney. Thank you, Father. David

How's the most beautiful girl in the world? David

This definition of a mystical dance comes from my heart, not a book. Tierney and I are entering into the great mystery of God Himself and it is our spirits, united with the Holy Spirit, that are dancing to God's song of love. It is not our flesh; it is our spirits that are uniting through the grace of God. That is why you are experiencing those moments in your body from afar as am I. You felt me there beside you tonight, in spirit. My eyes were closed and I was envisioning being there with you before you said it. It is ALL GRACE! I have never experienced anything like this before in my life. God is showing us the favor of His love beyond what I could have ever dreamed! Thank you, Father! I hope this sheds His light on what we are experiencing. We, through His grace have, in some way, entered into the great mystery of God. Your beloved. David

Thank you, Father, for this most amazing time of grace in my life. Father, I cannot believe that YOU have answered the prayer of my heart so PERFECTLY, so BEAUTIFULLY, all so preciously wrapped. Father, it will take me a lifetime of lifetimes to even begin to appreciate this most CHERISHED of Your hand-picked GIFTS (which you chose for me). Thank you, Father, and a very humble thank you to you, Tierney. I love you with an ever-deepening love that knows no bounds. David

Though oceans or continents or time zones may try to separate us, NOTHING can remove my greatest God-given treasure from my heart . . . you, Tierney. I am and always will be there for you! Your Beloved. David

Tonight, my love, I so yearn to hear the voice of your heart. It is the music of mine, sung by the sweetest, most delicious voice in the world! David

Your outward beauty captivated me, your inner beauty radiated to the very core of my soul . . . to the depths of my heart where NO ONE has ever penetrated. GIFTS . . . which You chose 4 me . . . Thank You Father . . . and a very humble THANK YOU 2 U TIERNEY . . . I LOVE YOU WITH AN EVER DEEPENING LOVE that knows no bounds. David

Good day, my gallant warrior. May the whisper of the Spirit prepare you today for the things ahead as God's ambassador. I do esteem you. XOX. Tierney

Thank you . . . it is the ECHO of my heart! The timing of the text was perfect. Tonight, my Dove, come perch in my branches and rest . . . then go deep into your nest within my heart, close your eyes, and allow me to shelter, protect, comfort, and envelope you with the pulsating warmth/heat of my ever-growing love for you! Your beloved. David

Thank u 4 sharing on the drive here . . . it brought me such great comfort . . . the ECHO of my heart!!!! David

I bet we could call that an "echocardiogram!" Tierney

You r too much . . . well actually just a perfect match/fit . . . physically, spiritually . . . a HANDCRAFTED PERFECT MATCH 4 MY HEART!!!! THANK YOU, FATHER! David

You are amazing. You are the perfect equation/recipe for a complex girl like me. Your drive and resolve mirrors mine. I love it. Tierney

Good morning my Dove . . . journaling our 4 days together has me awash with precious memories and moments . . . have a great day, your BELOVED. David

We r in business . . . got text, on plane . . . U r a great mystery I want to explore 4 the rest of my life . . . an ever deepening revelation of your RARE BEAUTY!!! Your Beloved, David

[22]Goooooood morning Vietnam!!! Good night my Love . . . miss u. David

Just a quick buzz to let you know you are in my heart and thoughts. I wish you were here to share the experience/adventure with me. You are awesome! I am proud of your business savvy. Luv it! David

By the way . . . I am ALL IN!!!! lifting u up in prayer . . . my beloved wish I was with YOU. David

Your energy excites me . . . u r an amazing woman . . . you make me feel like Adam must have felt when he awoke from his sleep and first set eyes on the PERFECT MATE GOD HAD CHOSEN 4 HIM . . . HE PROCLAIMED . . . WO-MAN . . . for God knew it was NOT good 4 man 2 be ALONE!!!! David

Lord, I stand and agree with my beloved . . . he can do all things through you who gives the strength and the power, for your grace is sufficient and in our weakness your strength is made strong. For your yoke is easy and your burden light. Tierney

Beam me up, Scotty! I am so all in . . . got a LOL moment sitting here all alone, going from an all-nighter {plane ride} to a five-hour meeting with my largest factory. Come, Holy Spirit, fill the heart of your faithful and kindle in me with the fire of your love. Use me as your instrument to penetrate the hearts of those you bring into my life this day. Speak through me, do not let me speak, and use me for your purpose. Be my strength, Lord. I belong to you. David

Believe me, I know without a doubt u could not only keep up but absolutely challenge me and I LOVE IT. David

Oh by the way, the cost of texting from Vietnam, my dear—YOU ARE WORTH ANY PRICE. David

"Love at first flight." (Quote by Tierney.) *I love it! David*

Arise, my beloved, my beautiful one and come. Let me hear your voice. You will have to give me the chance. How does that song go? Oh, yes, [23] "You ain't seen nothin' yet! Baby, you just ain't seen nothin' yet. Here's something you never gonna forget." David

I am so ALL in and the memories will keep getting deeper and richer all the days of our lives. Another ahhh moment! I am having so much fun. Thank you, my beloved. David

I am passionate about my love and commitment to you. Tierney

I forgot to tell you that the Spirit spoke to me yesterday and said, "Your business is NOT your life!" Ouch! I know, but it consumes me like it is. I am learning. Teach me. Tierney

Return hastily, oh my beloved and be like a gazelle or a young hart as you cover the mountains which separate us. She longingly addresses her absent shepherd. Tierney

Thank you, my protector and covering . . . may grace abound as you carry on your divinely-directed tasks . . . until the day breaks and shadows flee away. Tierney

I went through the same "letting go of His business," only with no one to support me—had the opposite. I am here for you and with you on your journey . . . it was in the letting go that He set me free and then He was able to use me for His purpose and glory. He chose to bless His business. David

You are my "Treasured Gift" from the King. David

You are my beloved and I will return to you with haste, taking you into my arms. I will drink from your wellspring of beauty and pour back into you the essence of my purified love. David

I could not help closing my eyes and seeing my Dove curled up in her nest. I pray to our Father for a heavenly breeze to sweep over her, enveloping her in peace, warmth, protection, and love. Father, may this cocoon of your heavenly grace be with Tierney throughout the night and go forth with her all the day. Please grant her in abundance the Gifts of the Spirit so that the fruits of her life's journey each day may bring you glory and may she, in abundance, experience the Fruits of the Holy Spirit. I pray this in the name of our Lord and Savior, Jesus Christ. David

I long to breathe into you the Breath of Life Who dwells within me and inhale from you the same. Your beloved. David

I experienced what God spoke to your heart yesterday . . . more tears, more healing. Thank you for being there for me. I wish I could just curl up in your arms, my head upon your chest, just above your heart, and hear what I am experiencing from you—the rhythm of true love. YHG {Your Humble Giant}. David

I see no risk, I see reward beyond measure. Thank you for this opportunity to woo your most precious heart. Your beloved. David

I absolutely love 2 text with u . . . talking to you, my preference over texting . . . being with you pales all the rest!!! Being with you, words alone cannot truly describe the Vast Ocean of emotions experienced those 4 irreplaceable days . . . love you my sweet. David

You are my hero Tierney!!! God has, is, and will use u in profound ways as His vessel 4 the salvation of souls . . . I am so honored 2 B part of your journey. David

Thx. These r our jewels in r crowns that we will throw at His feet one day. Tierney

I looked up "Phoenix" today . . . "universal symbol of the sun, mystical rebirth, resurrection, and immortality. It's a legendary fire bird believed to die in its self-made flames periodically each 100 years then rise again out of its own ashes." Significant. Tierney

The better thing that comes from trusting . . . it's so wonderful to be in God's perfect plan. I have never been surer that this love was worth waiting for. Thank you. Tierney

The rumor has it almost there . . . u have brought so much humor and laughter into my life . . . it is all part of the Phoenix rising, a new birth from the ashes. David

Has anyone told you yet today just how beautiful you are? Well, then this proclamation of this profound TRUTH comes to you all the way from Vietnam, special delivery, right to your heart! You are so beautiful. The mere thought of you takes my breath away. The vision causes my heart to skip a beat, and when I touch you (purely) . . . oh, my! A moment every sensory nerve in my body comes alive. "Beautiful" is only the starting word for the "treasure" of my life. My Dove, if you were here with me, you could snuggle into your nest. It is prepared only for you. You are the perfect fit. I hope this brightens your day. I so am in love with you. David

I felt your prayers, your affirmations, your presence in a very tender way. Thank you. Your wind in my sails and your essence in my heart . . . what more could any man ask for? David

Now that is thick! I am NOT all that . . . don't set yourself up 4 disappointment. Tierney

Sorry it was so thick . . . there is no dilution valve on the wellspring of my heart . . . you r the one that broke the seal . . . u r causing the flow. All I can do is slow up the volume . . . my precious key holder say the word and I will attempt the perilous task. Disappoint? Me!!! I think/know NOT. If you could only see what I see in u, u would totally agree. Remember I see multifaceted . . . every cut and layer of your beauty. I am the Jeweler of your heart . . . I do not only see the stunning beauty on the outside . . . I go deep 2 truly see all the brilliant colors emitted from every angle when you r exposed to the Light/Son. David

Is this the new Survivor series? Tierney (regarding David's trip).

Okay, David. I love you . . . it's for all your yes's. Tierney (what God spoke to my heart)

The first time Tierney held your hand, yes, at the airport. It felt so right, a perfect fit, so warm, so tender, so soft, yet secure. It was an exchange of tender, trusting, emerging phileo love. David

His ways r not our ways . . . His r always paved with peace . . . His plans 4 us r always much greater than our own. He knows the plans He has 4 us, they r MUCH GREATER than we have 4 ourselves . . . He is in control . . . we r in His Stream and I am luvin it . . . THANK YOU, FATHER. David

I love and respect your leadership skills. Wow! What a TEAM! God has joined us 4 a very special, anointed purpose . . . VERY SIGNIFICANT. David

We shared on the phone and God spoke to Tierney's heart about getting an annulment, even though she did not understand what it was, or what it meant. I shared all—the steps, process, and my desire for her to apply at the proper time. In reality, without it, I could not re-marry, could not go away from Christ or His Church. David

Thanks for your kind comments always. You are earning a lot of brownie points, you know. XOXO. You can save them and cash them in all at once. Tierney

I thought nothing should be this good. God reminded me of this Scripture: "The blessing of the Lord, it maketh rich, and He addeth no sorrow with it (Proverbs 10:22 KJV)." Thank you, Jesus. Tierney

You are right . . . I do not yet grasp your inner strength, your endurance. I am amazed that you care so much for me. I do not know why. I know my heart sings for you. I know your spirit more than your body and your voice. Tierney

It is not only my heart, but God's heart saying "thank you" for ALL you do for us. It is also for all of your yes's, Tierney, that you are experiencing this GIFT . . . a new springtime, a rebirth in the sacred life of the Trinity. The fingerprints of God are always an exchange of gifts. "You are both experiencing my love." David

I just came through Chinese customs and kept feeling your buzz in my briefcase. LOL. Your friend's confirmations are what I am experiencing. Those whose hearts are truly connected to the heart of Christ sing with the same voice—the voice of the Holy Spirit. The Holy Spirit NEVER contradicts itself—God's way of confirming that we are on the path. Anyone who perhaps is not in union with the consistent message is not a safe person to share with at this time. I have learned this in battle. YHG, David

As I have told you in the past, my love for you continues to grow richly, deeper, and its SIGNIFICANCE broadens with each day. What more could a man ask for? This is a very deep time of communal love. Luv ya! David

God just unveiled this to me . . . The first Catholic Mass I took you to was at St. Augustine's. (St. Augustine had an encounter with God at the beach when he tried to understand the Trinity. He came upon a little boy who was trying to empty the ocean into a hole he dug in the sand, bucket by bucket.) Now we are going to a town named St. Augustine's on our second get-together. Our next trip is to St. Michaels, the name of the archangel who defeated Satan and also who, I was told by a 14-year-old visionary in Ethiopia, would be in this battle with me. When I returned from this trip (Ethiopia) is when I was asked to move out.

This 14-year-old girl was driven six hours in the middle of the night by two nuns to bring me this message because the Lord instructed her to. Lastly, I evoked St. Michael last night when we talked (when I prayed). God's got us covered! He's sending us confirmation after confirmation . . . love you, beloved. David

Yes, leaving now. My assistant, when she texted back added, "your ship is coming in David." She has seen my pain. David

David Z. Abel . . . u may not c this until after u have climbed the wall . . . but u r such an amazing man . . . so Christ like! I have waited my whole life 4 the likes of u. Tierney

Your waiting is over, a new springtime has begun. The greatest adventure of our lives is before us. I am so ALL in. Never question the answer to the deepest prayer I have ever prayed. You are my treasured gift from God! Love ya! Besides, the room you are looking at needs some true heavenly beauty—YOU! All I see in this room is manmade stuff. David

Tierney, we are both growing, and growth always comes with pain. We are both dying to self so that it is He who lives in us, works through us, and is living with us. It is no longer we who live, but He who lives in us. In our humanity, we fall . . . then turn to God who understands, forgives, anoints, and empowers us to go forward again, without reservation. I love you . . . Your beloved. David

Words spoken to my heart for Tierney and me:
"My Son experienced rejection, scorning, betrayal, and chastisement from those He loved, and yet He still loved. You both are bringing my Son into the lives of others, so you, too, will experience what He experienced and your response must ALWAYS mirror His, which is love." David

I love you, Tierney. Thank you for being there for me . . . so sorry you cannot be all for everyone though you would be if you could. You are a treasure, Tierney. I long for the day when I can share ALL with you. You are my beloved "priceless treasure." David

This is "Sleepless in Beijing" reaching out with a heart touch to let you know that I am thinking about you. YHG, David

I was writing out our texts and wanted 2 comment on the Brownie points I am accumulating . . . you offered that I could cash them all in at once, however I would prefer, with your permission, 2 SAVOR the cashing in of each one, one by one, the rest of my life . . . AHHHHHHHH . . . MOMENTS OF BEAUTY . . . TREASURES OF THE PUREST INTIMACY . . . what more could a MAN OF GOD ask 4? I LOVE YOU TIERNEY . . . xoxoxo. David

At the top of the mountain at the Summer Palace in Beijing, China and I wanted to shout out: "I love you!" Your beloved. David

So you want to be a priest? Tierney

LOL . . . told you that was not my calling. It took one in seven billion to unlock this most sacred chamber of my heart . . . It took you! David

The script has been written and you have been chosen to sing the music of my "heart." You know the words, your fingers know the "keys," your body moves to the beat, so play away my Dove—the melodious music of my heart. I AM ALL YOURS. David

"I have both chosen and prepared this gift 4 u. All I ask of you is 2 accept the gift, TRUST IN ME (fear and doubt r not of Me) and give All your love 2 Me so that it is My Love that flows back through you 2 her/him," your Father. David

God is the Giver of every PERFECT gift. My mom just said she thinks you are relative material! I asked her to explain. She said because she approves of you. Tierney

It was spoken to both of us. "Trust in the Lord with ALL your heart. On your own intelligence rely not. In ALL your ways be mindful of Him, and He will make straight your paths. Honor the Lord with your wealth, with first fruits of all your produce. Then will your barns (soul) be filled with grain (the Bread of Life), with New Wine (Christ) your vats (hearts) will overflow. The discipline of the Lord distain not; spurn not His reproof. For whom the Lord loves, He reproves, and He chastises the son (daughter) He favors. {God spoke to me when He took me to these verses in my Bible. He "broke open" the "Bread of Life" for me.} The Father spoke to my heart: And with New Wine (My Son, Jesus), your vats (hearts) will overflow. The discipline of the Lord, my son (daughter), distain not; spurn not His reproof. I want to grow both of you in holiness and it will require you both to be open to learn, to be stretched, to change. Your ways are not my ways. Be open to My ways. I am in the cab on the way to the airport—almost there. Almost there with you, also . . . in your arms, captured by your lips. I surrender! I am so all in . . . captured and raptured into your heart. YHG, David (these words flowed from my heart).

"Will it last, Lord?" is the question of my heart. How can he/she be so perfect for me? Why do I, after all these many years of aching and yearning, find myself being offered the most perfect gift . . . the answer to my years of prayers without words, inner groanings that ONLY you could hear, Father. I do not feel worthy. "My child, I have heard your pleas. Not an utterance of your heart has escaped my ear. You are my son/daughter and I have both chosen and prepared this gift for you. All I ask of you is to accept the gift, TRUST IN ME (fear and doubt are not of me) and give ALL your love to me so that it is my love that flows back through you to her/him." David (heard from the Father—these words flowed from my heart as I texted them. They were for both of us).

My words to you, Tierney, echo the same . . . the heart of the giver is healing and just starting to overflow with the beauty of the love contained with the chamber to which you hold the only key. David

Do you know that it really makes me feel treasured and loved that u care . . . please do not stop . . . I may answer back from strength, however, you must realize that my strength in part comes from you . . . when you care, I TRULY feel LOVED . . . I LOVE YOU, TIERNEY. David

My dearest Tierney, my sweet, my love. I am so honored to be given this "once in a lifetime" opportunity to woo and court your most precious heart—true treasure of our King! I take this great honor on as the "quest of my life." As a trusted and gallant knight of the King's court, I will put on His armor, mount my stead, and ride, laying down my life, if necessary, to win your fair hand, my lady. And into my "castle keep" will I protect, nourish, adorn, and treasure your heart all the days of my life. So sleep, oh maiden fair. Let not the sound of the hoof beat of my steed awake you. Just sleep in His peace, knowing your knight rides! Your beloved. David

Please know this . . . in my attempt to be transparent, I never want to cause you to question my love for you and my commitment is to protect your beautiful heart and never have you question mine. I never want to hurt yours. Tierney

Thank you, God, for teaching me to laugh again, but please, Lord, don't ever let me forget that I cried. Tierney

Tierney's prayer before my talk: "We speak to you, oh enemy, and dismiss your power and hold on the hearts and lives of these men and release them to receive the Word of God. Father, we agree together that you will use your servant as your mouthpiece, that the oil of your anointing will pour forth and your Word will resound, accomplishing everything it sets out to do. Lord, convict and change hearts today with your heartbeat and the Holy Spirit. Give David clarity of mind and please use him mightily."

Perhaps it is good that we are lovers at a distance! Not! Tierney

I am ready, but by the grace of God and 1,000 unanswered questions that have to be faithed out. I so wish to be there with you now to walk the gardens with you. I would have a sense of wonder . . . I already do. Tierney

My love, this is one of the GREATEST awakenings of my life . . . second only 2 mine with God . . . U R MY PRICELESS TREASURE, MY HAND-BUILT, CUSTOM ORDERED, SPECIAL "AIR MAIL DELIVERY FROM THE KING!!!" The vault of my HEART is the ONLY SAFE PLACE in the world 2 safely store my life's most SIGNIFICANT GIFT from my Lord!!! Your Gallant Knight most humbly accepts this most prized possession in ALL the kingdom . . . the precious heart of the King's daughter. David

Thank u my love 4 unlocking, entering, and caring 4 this most vulnerable chamber of my heart . . . your tender touch is just what the Divine Physician ordered . . . tk u 4 being open 2 His request . . . I Love You . . . my precious Jewel . . . YHG, David

I am glad u r passionate and expressive. Happy u RSVPd to my garden invitation, MHG. While going thru my desert . . . I chose the word DREAM instead of anything else like . . . hope . . . love . . . resilience . . . etc. God has given me my dream deal . . . you! Tierney

I read your text and had a "MOMENT" THAT BUCKED MY KNEES!!!!! Wow . . . what u do 2 me, words cannot do justice!!! Tk u my love, my lover, my beloved. David

It is not heaven, however it is a foretaste, an ever so small sampling, a bite size morsel, of what is 2 come in the banquet of our life's journey. R u ready 4 the GREAT ADVENTURE? I do not want to experience it without uuuu—! David

Then there is NO turning back!!! The greatest adventure of our lives continues . . . books will b written of the journey to inspire hope, healing , and Love . . . the way it was meant 2 b . . . from the beginning . . . YHG, David

U are so adorable, asleep on a sofa . . . visual of OC {Ocean City}, if not physically, most certainly I am with you spiritually . . . I pray u and your family will experience a grace filled day/year w/our RISEN LORD . . . May He shower your family with blessings and the desires of your heart bloom with heavenly glory. The Master Gardener of your heart has prepared your soil, weeded, fertilized, planted, watered and put the SON so perfectly above it . . . this is a NEW SPRING TIME in your garden Tierney . . . thank you 4 the privilege, the honor, the opportunity, 2 slowly, gently, and with great care and reverence, enter your garden and drink in its breathtaking beauty and dazzling array of colors . . . This is a "ONCE IN A LIFETIME OPPORTUNITY." Thank you, my BELOVED . . . I greatly missed our sharing last night. David

Good morning, my Dove, I am listening 2 the sounds of springtime, outside my bedroom door + inside the chambers of my heart. Thk u 4 sharing your world w/me . . . esp. your sanctuary . . . Palm Island. I am so honored & blessed . . . the most favored among the King's Knights. David

Mornin, my S.O. . . . I am so favored 2 have your heart . . . best B'day gift a girl could imagine. May the Spirit lead u this day & use u 4 His purposes with those who labor among + with u my valiant warrior. Xoxox. Tierney

MHG . . . I am igniting the fire of the Holy Spirit in u & expecting His words to flow. I love u . . . hear the whoosh of the Spirit beneath your sails . . . His and mine. Tierney

I got your anniversary card . . . oh my . . . I am sooo blessed . . . u r the "SCRIPT" of my heart . . . down 2 the finest detail!!! U R my BELOVED. David

Truly my pleasure, your script is a MASTERPIECE that will take a lifetime of in-depth, personal study 2 truly begin to grasp the depth of its FULL beauty . . . I AM ALL IN 4 THE LIFELONG ADVENTURE. YHG, David

I so long to be fully in your life. I am missing you. I am experiencing such an ache, like I am incomplete. You complete me, my perfect complement. I so enjoy sharing my life with you that it is no longer mine but OURS. I wish I were with you. We would laugh and dance 'til the sun came up in the morning and found us curled up in each other's arms in a hammock under the trees, my dearest Tierney. I LOVE YOU! He is making ALL things NEW. His plan for us is PERFECT! Full of life. He {God} is the Author of the DANCE our united hearts yearn for . . . YHG, David

I know . . . not to minimize all that but I hate "in between." I hate wasted time & yet I know the Sovereignty of God. I am tired of waiting . . . obviously patience is not my virtue here. Practically speaking . . . I am ready 2 get on with it . . . to grasp the commission . . . I don't like all the questions unanswered . . . the how's, the when's . . . sorry! Let's hope it's only hormones. Spent my life waiting . . . don't want to miss another moment. UGH! Just spouting off. It will be ok—just need the grace but want the understanding . . . u know me. Tierney

Good morning my Dove, awoke 2 the beauty + melody of a new springtime . . . I drifted through our treasure trove of memories . . . Pure JOY swept over me. David

I am at church by myself, walking the Passion of Christ {stations of the Cross}, and when I looked at the fourth image, a "Daughter of God the Father" comforting His Son on His journey to Calvary, God spoke this to my heart: "As I sent My daughter to comfort My Only Begotten Son, Jesus, as He carried His cross, so too, David, I have sent my daughter, Tierney, to comfort you and tend to your wounds. Be at peace, my son. I love you." David

U r being used so mightily . . . I love the "wing-side" seat. I adore you. Tierney

I would suffer ALL the pains all over again, just 2 b w/u . . . u were soooo worth the journeys of agony and purification . . . u r my ONE, my ONLY, my FIRST. David

My heart beats for you, my beloved. Long have I waited for this moment in time—for the music of the mystical dance of love, for my chosen partner to unlock the chambers of my heart so that they may flow freely with the nectar of love. You are my beloved, my bride-to-be. Drink freely from the springs of my heart—I have both given and entrusted it to you. Bathe in the waters of its beauty. They flow for you and you alone. YHG, David

Beauty such as yours is entrusted 2 only the 1 that can truly cherish it . . . the luster of your beauty, my love, will take a lifetime 2 fully absorb. I am sooo all in. YHG, David

My dearest Heavenly Father, may I please be given the grace to greet each new day's dawning, as the birds do, with melodious songs of joy, thanksgiving, praise, gratitude, and worship to You, Father, and may the voice that unites with mine be the voice of Tierney Hathaway Foster's. I love You, Father. This is my heart's deepest desire. My dearest Heavenly Father, You are making everything new. You are in control. I am so thankful, so grateful, so humbled at what You are doing in my life, and most importantly, whom You have entrusted to my care—Your daughter, Tierney. Oh my Father, such a treasure as this a man could invest his whole life searching for and never find this Treasure of Treasures, and yet You have chosen me to receive this gift of a lifetime. Please Father, grant me the grace to love her as You love her, cherish her as You cherish her, honor her as You honor her ALL the days of my life. Your beloved son, David.

Way 2 much road wear for my warrior . . . come + sit a spell w me . . . download everything . . . let me massage yr head, feet & back . . . Let me let u b mindless 4 a while . . . I hope u r not driving . . . I'm tired just thkg abt it. Tierney

I need u around u know . . . u must be Built to Last or I will be so undone again. Tierney

Oh I'm built 2 last . . . not driving, doing book work . . . Oh, baby I am so ALL IN!!!! Wow . . . did I enjoy your text . . . I'm yours my love. . . . YHG, David

Good morning my love . . . I sooooo enjoyed our sharing last night . . . it was almost like I was with u . . . u r my soulmate my love . . . thank u for opening up your heart 2 me. I will never take it for granted . . . I will always nurture, cherish, protect, and woo this most tender part of u. YHG, David

Thank u Tierney my love . . . I so long 2 b united w/u, 2 experience this great adventure of life TOGETHER . . . love u sweetheart. David

Just looked at your picture I have in my planner . . . ahh . . . so beautiful . . . so swweeeet, soooo my treasure. Wow! Cannot wait 2 see u again. David

Wow . . . HAPPY ANNIVERSARY MY LOVE, I will be on a plane flying east 4 4hrs filled w/memories of our first meeting!!!! SWEET TREATS . . . I LOVE U MY BELOVED. David

Do u know + feel how deeply I LOVE YOU??? I pray so . . . 4 life would b incomplete + soooo less fulfilling without u . . . u r precious 2 me Tierney!!!!! David

Mom is good, sitting here now showing her the pictures . . . wow, I just opened 1 of u + I. OH MY, LOOK AT THE BEAUTY ON MY ARM. WOW!!!! Luv u sweetheart. David

Treasured, cherished, and precious are the memories I have stored in the vault of my heart of us. Their value is priceless because money can neither buy nor replace them. Their significance has no earthly measure but rather, a heavenly origin. Books will be written to tell our story, my love. They will impact countless numbers as their message of hope, healing, redemption, and true love, as it was meant to be, pierces the heart of the reader. I love you, my beloved. Thank you, Father, for entrusting to me the heart of your most precious daughter. David

I miss u so deeply my love, I'm so very grateful 4 the time we have together . . . u make every day brighter. Every moment we share sweetens this great adventure. David

Not long ago we were in the Emergency Room with separate issues yet similar symptoms. Whew! Today we are in the Waiting Room together. It is a much better place to be! I love you! Tierney

U r always w/me my love, I carry U in the sanctuary of my heart. Whenever I choose 2 go there it is so refreshing, so life-giving, the fragrance soothes my very soul. I go there often throughout my day . . . I love you my Dove. David

Thank u 4 yr promises. I am impatient but learning the disciplines of waiting 4 His timing . . . not gracefully but with my knee bent. It's hard to be in the closet!! Tierney

I love you . . . if I was Ruth, u would be my Boaz. Tierney

Just so you know that I am grateful for every chance we have to touch base. I will NEVER hold you hostage with expectations. Will I miss you? Terribly! Hope vball was a releaser. I luv u. Tierney

Good morning, my love. I wish I were there 2 slowly awake w/u. Treasured + significant was this time we were together. Your boys r amazing young men. I miss you. David

Brit says thx . . . he said it is almost 2 good 2 b true. That u r everything he would have asked for me. Tierney

I have entrusted u with my heart, 2 no other has this gift been presented fully, completely, without reservation . . . it is yours Tierney. May God the Father join our 2 hearts in the mystical dance of Love, God's love. David

I miss you sweetheart. I'm going into the treasure trove of our memories & it is setting my heart on fire. Love David—YHG

To my love . . . I hope u find this in the a.m. U r above all men, most amazing. How did I get so blessed? Certainly it is unmerited favor! I wish I could pop in this wkend. Alas! If we chg dates 4 Ireland, any chance of u scooting in earlier? Now it feels like a long time away, doesn't it? I always said no long distance relationships again . . . never say never! U r so worth it. Tierney

Tell me it will always be like this. Tierney

Watch my actions . . . they speak the truth of my heart . . . u r my beloved. David

Love U my Dove, the nest of my arms yearn 4 u, the warmth of my heart pines 2 comfort, cherish & woo you this day and all the days of my life. David

Oh baby, there is no changing my mind 4 my love 4 u is from the depths of my heart where God lives, not my head. I am responding 2 His music & invitation 2 court his daughter. David

Just praying 4 us. My former asst said we looked like bro & sis in pix . . . she said our story should become a movie . . . hmmm.. I'll have 2 read the last chapter to c! Tierney

Sweetheart we ain't seen nothin' yet . . . our eyes have not seen yet the great adventure the Lord has in store for us!!!! David

Just as this plant bursts forth its beauty in vibrant colors so 2 is my heart for you. David

Good day my valiant warrior . . . today, take this power for all u have to accomplish. I'm in your wing-side seat blowing in yr sails. I love u. Tierney

Thank u 4 yr msgs . . . so this is the 1st time u have had a temperature warning? I thk that should have come a lot sooner! HOT HOT HOT SIZZLE. LOL. Tierney

Whoops . . . sorry . . . I just want u to know how secure I am under yr left arm & yr protection. Thk u 4 yr prayers & yr love always. U r such an amazing man. Thks 4 being mine. Tierney

Awe . . . one can dream . . . I'm good at that. Tierney

I am hopelessly in love with you. Tierney

[24] "How do I love thee? Let me count the ways." I believe it will take me a lifetime 2 count all the ways I love u. Will you stay w/me so that I may show u all the ways? Know that it will take a lifetime. YHG, David

I so miss your beauty, your touch, your joy, the melody of your sweet voice, the warmth + comfort of your embrace, and the soft inviting kiss of your lips . . . most of all I so deeply miss your heart/you. Your beloved. David

I am so anxious 2 share my life w/u my love!!!!!No more lonely nights. David

My love, come into my arms and snuggle. Kiss me like there is no tomorrow. I miss u. I ache 4 your tender touch. David

Good morning, my love. You r such a light + source of great joy!!!! U cause my cheeks to hurt as you bring me laughter. Cannot wait 2 talk to u tonight, perhaps. David

U have spent yr energies celebrating others, my privilege is to celebrate u! It is among my highest callings + I am so excited. Tierney

I am so blessed, so loved, by the most beautiful woman in the WORLD!!!! The script of my heart . . . YOU my love!!!!! Ahhhhh! David

My love, my tanks r full and overflowing. My memory banks r spilling forth memories that NO amount of money can buy . . . They r precious, they r treasured, they r life giving, they r sacred; God ordained. I love u Tierney. David

I ache for my partner. Sleep numbs the pain of our separation. Hope warms my heart . . . missing you. David

Be at peace, my love. I will walk it with you . . . we will walk it together. It is part of our journey, part of our story, our testimony that God will use to help others. It will build our faith and trust in God. You are my beloved, chosen by Mary, ordained by God, led by the Spirit, and united in Christ. YHG, David (regarding the length of time for the annulment).

My Dove, the nest of my heart so yearns to be with you. This time of separation grows the ever-present ache to be united with you. YHG, David

My love, I can almost taste the sweetness of that holy day when God the Father makes all things new. We will be united in His garden which He created for us. We will walk with God in a very special, very sacred way. He will use us to breathe hope into the broken-hearted and the weary sojourner of the world. David

My love, there are peaks and valleys along our journey that we will travel together. We will learn, we will grow, and we will dance the dance of life united. David

Good morning, my sweet man . . . alive with the Holy Spirit, touched by the Father, loved by Mother Mary, adored by this handmaiden. Tierney

My Dove, I ache to be in your arms, to feel our souls joined in God's embrace, united as one, inseparable in a holy union. YHG, David

You push yourself so hard for everyone else. I want to provide a place of rest and protection for you. Your life is a drink offering that is poured out for many. Tierney

My beloved, my heart burns with an unquenchable fire of love for you. David

My sleeping giant, I count my blessings all day long and all night long. I dream of you and the day we won't have to leave each other's embrace. Tierney

My "Energizer Bunny," you make me quake to my very core! It is an electrifying experience that I have never felt before. My heart yearns for you each morning. I awake, my love. You are the "One," the perfect match, the perfect fit, hand-crafted by the hand of the Father, my true love. Your David.

"Sweet"—the music of hearts beating in unison. We are a perfect fit/match. Mother Mary chose the perfect soul mate for me. A mother always knows best. The enemy is raging because he does not want to see us united in Christ. He wants to steal our joy and wound our hearts. I say he has no power. Christ has won. Let us stay in the Garden and walk with God. Your David.

Do you know how proud I am of you, your choices, your character, and how God is using you so profoundly, my humble giant? Tierney

Who is giving credence to the enemy's attempt to distract us from our gaze and focus on Christ, causing us to sink into his muck and mire? Our faith is in our Lord who is our life and our first love. He is playing the music within our hearts. It is the mystical dance of love. Let us help each other tune out the static of the enemy whose mission is to divide and destroy what the Lord is doing and to steal our joy. I am your beloved. David

"Fixing our eyes on the Author and Finisher of our faith." "He who waits upon the Lord shall renew his strength; he shall mount up with wings as an eagle. He shall run and not be weary; he shall walk and not faint." Tierney

My dearest sweet man . . . your Mother Mary has been pouring out her heart for you into mine this morning. She is giving me the sense of your tenderness right now, the load on your heart. I am with you, my love. She also asked me if I realized how privileged my calling to you is and that my heart for my children was like hers. I had to apologize for my lack of understanding and my cynicism where she was concerned in my doctrine and thinking. I am understanding the necessary submission of our hearts and lives in order to walk out the calling on our lives, His timing, and His ways. I cannot explain it, but my spirit is receiving these messages. I am honored. Tierney

My spirit is reaching your spirit today and I am doing warfare as I am prompted. It is in the heavenlies now. The spirit is trying to reign down answers and there is a battalion of evil forces trying to prevent it. Tierney. {Tierney told me the name of the enemy was "Legion."}

Dream the dream of your heart . . . the Father is listening. David

I was just getting ready to write to you . . . 365 days ago I met the most remarkable man. In all my 40+ years as a believer, I have never met a more Christ-like man. I am so very blessed to have his heart. I do not know why me, but I am forever grateful to my heavenly Father for appointing such a guardian/caretaker of my life. Thank you, Lord! Thank you, David! I love you, My Humble Giant. Happy Anniversary! Tierney

Happy Anniversary, my Dove! The nest of my heart belongs to you. It is a custom fit, made by the Father for His precious daughter. You, my beloved, are the "one." Mother Mary knew the perfect match for her son . . . a beloved disciple who stands beside her at the foot of the cross that bears the "fruit of her womb." She is the "new Eve" who offers us now the fruit from the "Tree of Life" (the cross), her Son, Jesus Christ, the "New Adam." We have been allowed to enter the Garden, eat of the fruit of the "Tree of Life" and walk with God, the Father, in a very special way as a foretaste of heaven. I love you, my beloved. David

Revelation 12:17 NABRE: *"Then the dragon became angry and went off to wage war against the rest of her offspring, those who keep God's commandments and bear witness to Jesus."*

That's you and me, my Dove. The war is raging all around us, but when we look with our spiritual eyes, we see the armies of God, the heavenly hosts doing battle for us. God is uniting us for a VERY SPECIAL purpose. YHG, David

Oh my beloved. Dear, sweetness of my morning's awaking, oh how I long 4 the day when we will be united in Holy Matrimony. How long my Lord, how long? We humbly await your timing, because it is perfect. We are so very grateful for what U r doing in our lives & on our hearts. With hearts filled w/gratitude we come. David

My beloved I ache 2 breathe in your beauty. I long 2 b your husband. I cherish our time together. I treasure your heart. I'm not perfect and I'm sorry 4 the times I have gone ahead of u. Be patient w/me love. The Lord is at work in me. Please Lord, love YOUR beloved through me. YHG, David

I'm so honored & humbled that u chose me. Tk u Father 4 this most treasured gift, the precious heart of your daughter. David

WOW!!! What a most amazing dress!!!! U will look STUNNING. I'm so excited!!! TK U, Father. Tk U Tierney. Good morning my Dove. The nest of my heart awaits. David

Baby, U r filling my heart w/such anticipation!!!! I'm a teenager, a bridegroom, a man who God has chosen to entrust His most precious gift with, His daughter. WOW! I'm the most blessed man in the world. Love u DOVE. David

I do feel secure with you and I trust you which is nothing that comes easy for suspicious me (remember, I pre-qualify everything). Tierney

Father, how can I thank you for this amazing gift? She is all the desires of my heart all wrapped up in the cutest package. I could not have imagined it possible that you answered the ache of my heart down to the finest detail. I love you, Father. David

"Accept the gift, David. She was chosen for you."

Tierney gave me this precious picture of her getting made up in the mirror. She was a princess then; she is a queen now, my queen. I will lay down my life for her. David

Tierney told me God told her to tell me: *"This is your time, David. It is for you."* My moment.

Your beauty permeates my every sense to my very core. You arouse the inner man within me. You make me feel like a man. You are my Eve, created by God, the Father, chosen by Mother Mary as my suitable partner, my help meet. You are my beloved. Your David.

On Our Wedding Day:
Good morning, my beloved! Today is the day the Lord has made and ordained to be a day of celebration, of rejoicing, of thanksgiving, of dancing. The bridegroom is calling, come my beloved, this is our day to give testimony to the love story scripted from our hearts, penned there by the Father, unveiled by the Mother, and lived out through the Son. I am yours, my Dove. May our Lord Jesus Christ love you purely through me all the days of your life and eternally with Him. YHG, David

Anticipation and love for the next chapter of our great adventure!!!! Just breathe love. This is our day. It is/will be "PERFECT." David

I will wrap u in the mantle of my protection & fill u w/the very essence of my soul. David

As Adam awoke from his sleep to proclaim truth when he saw his helpmate for the first time, "WOMAN," so too do I proclaim this amazing TRUTH. "WooooMAN" U take my breath away . . . u make me feel like a real MAN. David

I love you, my Dove. The nest of my heart yearns to be filled with your beauty. You ignite a fire within my heart that can be seen by heaven itself as it is fueled by the fire of Divine love—a God story like none other. You are the treasure of my heart. Thank you for dancing the dance of life with me. Thank you, Father, for the gift of your beloved daughter's heart. I will cherish it all the days of my life. YHG, David

NOTES

[1]Roberts, Frances J. *Come Away My Beloved*. Uhrichsville, OH: Barbour Pub., 2002. Print.

[2]Chapman, Steven Curtis. *Beauty Will Rise*. One Blue Petal Music, 2009. CD.

[3]Chapman, Gary D. *The Five Love Languages: The Secret to Love That Lasts*. Chicago: Northfield Pub., 2010. Print.

[4, 5]Chapman, Steven Curtis. *Beauty Will Rise*. One Blue Petal Music, 2009. CD.

[6]National Enquirer. "Enquiring Minds Want to Know." 1987. Trademarked phrase.

[7]Oliver, Mary. "The Summer Day." *House of Light*: Beacon Press, 1990. N. pag. Print.

[8]Albom, Mitch. "Every ending is just a new beginning that we fail to realize at the time." 2004. Quote.

[9]*The Five People You Meet in Heaven*. Dir. Lloyd Kramer. Prod. Mitch Albom. Perf. Jon

Voight, Ellen Burstyn, Jeff Daniels, Dagmara Dominczyk, Michael Imperioli. Hallmark Entertainment, 2004. DVD.

[10]Chapman, Gary D. *The Five Love Languages: The Secret to Love That Lasts.* Chicago: Northfield Pub., 2010. Print.

[11]Eggerichs, Emerson. *Love & Respect: The Love She Most Desires, the Respect He Desperately Needs.* Nashville, TN: Integrity, 2004. Print.

[12, 13]Eldredge, John. *Wild at Heart: Discovering the Secret of a Man's Soul.* Nashville, TN: Thomas Nelson, 2001. Print.

[14]Chapman, Steven Curtis. *Beauty Will Rise.* One Blue Petal Music, 2009. CD.

[15]West, Christopher, and John Paul. *Sacramental Sexuality an Overview of the Theology of the Body.* Our Father's Will Comm., 2001. CD.

[16]Barnard, Frederick R. "A picture is worth a thousand words." Printer's Ink, 1921. Quote.

[17, 18, 19]West, Christopher, and John Paul. *Sacramental Sexuality an Overview of the Theology of the Body.* Our Father's Will Comm., 2001. CD.

[20]Gray, Alice. "Let Go and Let God." *Stories for the Heart: Over 100 Stories to Encourage Your Soul.* Sisters, OR: Multnomah, 1996. N. pag. Print.

[21]Peyton, Father Patrick, The Rosary Priest. "The family that prays together stays together." N.d. Quote.

[22]*Good Morning, Vietnam.* Dir. Barry Levinson. By Mitch Markowitz. Perf. Robin Williams, Forest Whitaker. Buena Vista Pictures Distribution, 1987. Videocassette.

[23]Bachman, R., and B. Thornton. *You Ain't Seen Nothin' Yet; Free Wheelin'.* Mercury, 1974. Vinyl recording.

[24]Browning, Elizabeth Barrett, and Miroslava Wein. Dow. "How Do I Love Thee? Let Me Count the Ways." *A Variorum Edition of Elizabeth Barrett Browning's Sonnets from the Portuguese.* Troy, NY: Whitston Pub., 1980. N. pag. Print.